PRE-GAME

*"The wisest decisions aren't made by choosing one over the others—
they're made by honoring all three: head, guts, and heart."*

—Sherry Levin

"Coach Sherry Levin has lived it. The dreaming, the scheming, the falling down, the getting back up . . . In "Pre-Game--A Winning Mindset," she shares what it's like to be in the cauldron stretching--always stretching-- for a bar that's slightly out of reach. You'll find yourself tip-toeing to touch higher as you read!"

—Sherri Coale, Author, Speaker,
Hall of Fame Women's Basketball Coach

"Sherry Levin is a living, breathing source of inspiration. Pre-Game is a life's manual to getting through life with courage, love, community and strength. Each chapter leads you to the next phase of life, reminding you that you have the power to choose your next play. I was lucky enough to be coached by Sherry Levin and her pre-game speeches changed my life forever—I'm positive this book will change your life."

—Laticia Rolle, Model; Founder, Tress Hats; Actress; Podcaster

"Pre-Game isn't just a must-read for coaches and athletes—it's a playbook for life. Whether you are preparing for a big game or facing a personal crossroad, Pre-Game offers sharp insights, real world strategies, and a fresh perspective on how to show up with clarity, purpose and resilience. It goes beyond sport, reminding us that the mindset we build before we step onto the court is the same one we need to face life's toughest moments. Sherry's insights are invaluable for anyone looking to shift their mindset."

—Brenda Frese, University of Maryland Women's Basketball
Head Coach, National Champions of 2006, 650+ wins in twenty-three years at
Maryland, Two-time National Coach of the Year

"Right up my alley, aces!! Pre Game is a Game changing experience that provides the cheat code too and inspires that winning frame of mind. It transcends sport into winning at life. A positive perspective that's able to ignite the fire of success."

—Chris Collins, Longtime Sportscaster

"Coach Sherry didn't just prepare me for games, she honestly prepared me for life. Her lessons about mindset, resilience, and belief shaped the athlete I became and the woman I continue to grow into. This book captures the same wisdom she poured into me every single day."

—Oluchi Okananawa, Current University of Maryland player,
Duke University 2023-2025, Worcester Academy graduate 2023

PRE-GAME

A WINNING MINDSET

SHERRY LEVIN

PRE-GAME

A Winning Mindset
by Sherry Levin

First Edition
Copyright © 2026

Published by
Munn Avenue Press
300 Main Street, Ste 21
Madison, NJ 07940
MunnAvenuePress.com

For permission requests, contact MunnAvenuePress.com

Paperback ISBN: 978-1-969679-33-9
Hardcover ISBN: 978-1-969679-34-6

Printed in the United States of America

I dedicate this compilation to all the players I have coached throughout the years. Some of them "got it" immediately, and some it took years before they looked back and said, "Ahhhh, Coach Levin was right! Now I see." Those are the special players who motivate me every day.

To my supporters around every turn... You know who you are.

To Coach Togo Palazzi, who motivated me every day. He would motivate and inspire me with his booming voice, kindness, love of the game, and his grandiose quotes. One of his favorites that hung in our locker room was a quote by Vince Lombardi:

> *"Winning is not a sometime thing; it's an all the time thing. You don't win once in a while... You don't do things right once in a while... You do them right all the time. Winning is a habit. Unfortunately, so is losing."*

Togo told me the story of when he asked his Holy Cross coach and mentor, Buster Sheary, what he could do to repay Coach Sheary for all he had done for him. Togo heartfully repeated what Buster said, "Do it for someone else." I always thought that I was Togo's "someone else."

To my mom, who professes she is "not a reader," I hope she reads this one. Thank you for all your love and support throughout my life. My dad passed away in 2009, and I still think of him every day. He was my hero and gave me the confidence to be myself, to love sports, and to pursue my dreams with passion.

And of course, to my absolute joy in life, my daughter Marcia. She is everything to me. My heart and soul, my rock, my belly laugh partner, and my oxygen. THIS IS FOR YOU!

Love you all!

A NOTE TO THE READER

I would like to thank the real-life people who have made such an impact on my life: my mentors, teammates, coaches, players, and colleagues. Your influence has shaped not only my career but also the person I've become. The stories and experiences shared in this memoir are based on my personal recollections and interpretations of events as I experienced them. Memory is inherently subjective, and others who were present may remember these moments differently. I have done my best to capture the essence and spirit of these experiences as they unfolded in my life. Some names, identifying details, and timelines may have been altered or condensed to protect privacy and to serve the narrative flow of the book. Any errors or misremembering are unintentional and entirely my own.

This book is not intended as a definitive account of events, but rather as a sharing of my journey and the lessons I've learned along the way. My hope is to offer meaningful perspectives on viewing life through a positive lens and strategies for shifting one's mindset toward growth and success.

The views and opinions expressed in this memoir are solely my own and do not necessarily reflect those of any individuals, organizations, or institutions mentioned within these pages.

FOREWORD

by Laticia Rolle

I can still remember the way it felt sitting in the locker room before a big game, the air thick with nerves, sneakers squeaking against the floor as we paced, waiting for Coach Levin to come in. And then she'd arrive, calm yet powerful, her eyes steady, her outfit ready, her words clear. She didn't just talk about plays or matchups—she spoke of heart, resilience, and belief. She told us we had a choice in how we showed up that day, no matter who was on the other side of the court. Her words lit a fire in us, and when we hit the floor, it wasn't just basketball we were playing—it was a reflection of who we were becoming.

At the time, I thought those pre-game speeches were simply about winning games. But years later, I realized they were the blueprint for how I'd navigate my entire life.

There was one game in particular I'll never forget. We were down at halftime, frustrated and unsure. Coach walked in and looked at each of us—not with disappointment, but with belief. She reminded us that the scoreboard didn't define us, but our response did.

"What matters is the next play," she said.

"You Can. And you will."

We went back out, locked in, and fought with everything we had. That mantra—focus on the next play—became a thread I've carried into every part of my life since.

When I stepped into the world of entrepreneurship, and things didn't go as planned, I remembered that locker room. When doors closed on me in modeling, when rejections piled up, I remembered her voice: Next play. When I launched my podcast and felt the weight of doubt, wondering if my voice mattered, I leaned into the confidence she had instilled in me. Over and over, Coach Levin's words reminded me that setbacks aren't the end—they're just a moment, a chance to choose again, to keep going, to rise.

Beyond the wins and losses, what Coach taught us most was the power of the team. She showed us that real strength is built in community, that we are always better together. The camaraderie I felt with my teammates, rooted in her leadership, became the foundation of the communities I've built throughout my life. Whether in business, in creative spaces, or in sisterhood, I've carried her lesson that success is not about individual achievement, but about lifting others alongside you.

That is the brilliance of this book. *Pre-Game: A Winning Mindset* is more than a collection of lessons—it's the feeling of being in that locker room again, ready to take the court, hearing Coach remind you that you already have what it takes. Each chapter is a huddle before life's big moments, urging you to choose courage, to lean into love, and to find strength in your people.

This is a book for athletes, yes—but it's also for anyone who has ever faced doubt, fear, or obstacles that felt too big to overcome. It's for entrepreneurs chasing dreams, students trying to find their path, parents raising families, and anyone who could use a reminder that they are stronger than they know. As I reflect on my journey—from athlete to entrepreneur, model, and podcaster—I can see how deeply those locker room lessons shaped me. They gave me resilience when life felt heavy. They built my confidence when the world tried to shake it. They gave me motivation when I questioned if I could keep going. And above all, they reminded me that life, like basketball, is not just about winning—it's about how you show up, how you support your team, and how much of your heart you're willing to give.

Coach Levin's voice has been a compass in my life, and I know it will become one in yours, too.

Laticia Rolle was a Worcester Academy graduate in 2006. She led the way to our undefeated season in 2006 and the New England Preparatory School Athletic Council (NEPSAC) Championship. Laticia is now a model, entrepreneur, podcaster, and actress.

TABLE OF CONTENTS

MY WHY

Bounce, bounce, pause, bounce, quiet, swoosh! Repeat...

The snap of rubber against a polished hardwood floor. The sharp squeak of a sneaker breaking traction. The pregnant pause. The unmistakable swoosh of the ball passing through the net.

When I close my eyes, I hear the sounds of the game echoing through my mind. Basketball has been a part of my life for over fifty years. Without it, I would not be who I am today. The lessons one has to learn in order to last in a world where you spend every moment in direct competition with someone else, and stay a positive person, are the kind that will define you. The kind that you will take with you in any challenge, no matter where and when you face it, whether they come from hard-won championship matches, devastating losses, or quiet moments with your team on the road. I feel incredibly lucky to have lived a life so full of inspiration as both a player and as a coach, and the chance to share the lessons I've learned is something I consider another gift.

Pre-Game: A Winning Mindset is more than just a book of accumulated basketball pre-game speeches—it's a guide to transforming everyday moments, both simple and complex, into powerful sources of inspiration. The speeches will show you how to shift your perspective, turning negative feelings into opportunities for growth and positivity. The lens through which you view the world can be the key to turning even the toughest situations into something meaningful. This is not just a "how-to" book; it's a blueprint for living life fully.

Since my earliest childhood memories, I have been in love with sports. It didn't matter which ones. It didn't matter if I played or watched. I can remember being glued to the television for a big Friday Night Fight with my dad, watching Muhammad Ali vs. Frazier with Howard Cosell as the announcer. Or sitting in our comfy chair on a

Saturday afternoon, watching *Wide World of Sports* or the football or basketball game of the week. If there was a sporting event on television, I was watching it.

We watched live as we witnessed part of history, such as the unspeakable terrorist attack in Munich at the 1972 Olympics. On the other side of monumental sporting events, we rushed home from basketball practice to witness the 1980 Miracle on Ice when the men's Team USA hockey team beat the Soviet Union. On the one day a year when the Association for Intercollegiate Athletics for Women's basketball championship was on PBS, I marked it in red on my calendar. I was also lucky to attend every professional game my dad bought tickets to. Growing up in proximity to Boston, you can imagine just how much of a Celtics, Bruins, Red Sox, and Patriots fan I am, right to the core.

My competitive nature shaped my perspective, driving me to view situations through a win-or-lose lens, with an unwavering determination to strive for victory in everything I approached. So reading *Pre-Game: A Winning Mindset* is deeply personal and powerfully uplifting. This book meets readers where they are—no matter what challenges they face—and equips them with practical tools, real-life lessons, and a new perspective to approach any situation with clarity and positive intellect. Through special cues and insights, readers will discover how to turn negative situations into opportunities for growth and self-empowerment.

Each pre-game speech shares a real-life experience, reframed as a lesson designed to help readers make intentional, positive choices in their lives. These stories resonate deeply, offering a fresh lens through which to view their struggles and challenges while sparking hope, motivation, and readiness to move forward. The locker room is a sacred place to me—a sanctuary where coaches and players find their purpose.

With your eyes, your heart, and your mind wide open, you will:

✓ **Feel Empowered:** Recognize your inner strength and ability to navigate life's hurdles with confidence and optimism.

✓ **Gain Perspective:** Learn to view your challenges as opportunities for growth and see yourself handling tough situations with grace and wisdom.

✓ **Be Energized:** Draw energy and inspiration from the book's relatable stories and actionable strategies, feeling ready to take on the game of life with renewed purpose.

✓ **Take Action:** Be ready to apply the lessons and mindset shifts immediately, using the pre-game cues to tackle obstacles and make positive changes in your life.

Ultimately, *Pre-Game: A Winning Mindset* empowers you to transform your mindset into a muscle you can rely on—a source of strength, resilience, and inspiration for whatever comes next. You'll walk away energized by my perspective, ready to choose a positive path no matter the situation.

Nature or nurture? For me, it was a resounding combination. When I was very young, I earned the nickname "Monkey" because I liked to climb on all the jungle gym equipment in the playground. I can remember in elementary school playing tackle football with the boys during recess, much to the chagrin of my mom, who loved to clothe me in dresses. I played street hockey in the parking lot and would challenge the fastest of the boys to a 50-yard dash on the field. I would win. I played Four Square and even King of the Mountain, where we would try to knock down the kid on top of the ten-foot snow banks. I was always eager to jump into the Bulldog version of the game of tag, where you tackled the slower kids as they ran by.

Basketball became my first love in high school, above soccer, track and field, and playing the clarinet. My freshman summer, I had signed up for a local basketball camp, and at the last minute, my friend who had signed up with me could not attend. Naturally, as a teenage girl, the thought of going to a camp without knowing anyone was horrifying, so I told my parents, "Well, I am not going either." They, of course, said, "No way. You are going. You will make new friends." I did attend. I made new friends, and I won multiple awards, including Most Outstanding Player. I was hooked! Lesson learned.

That basketball camp would change the course of my life. I saw Togo Palazzi as a guest lecturer. I was enthralled by his intensity and motivation. I knew at that moment, sitting under the center hoop in the front row, that Togo was the type of coach I wanted to play for. And not only would

I play for a dynamic, inspiring, and knowledgeable coach like Togo, as fate would have it, I played *for* Togo.

I was introduced to Holy Cross because of Togo. Yes! Did I mention he was named to be the women's head coach while I was deciding where to attend college on a scholarship? Timing is everything, and my choice was a good one. I still hold the all-time scoring record with 2,253 points and won eighty-two games while losing just twenty-one of the games I played. And now my jersey hangs in the rafters of the Hart Center at Holy Cross, and the Sherry Levin Women's Basketball Lounge is named for me. I could not have done any of this without surrounding myself with supportive friends, teammates, my family and the trust of those pushing me. All these experiences have led me here.

After graduating from college, I knew I wanted to pursue a career in broadcasting. Fortunately, I had the incredible opportunity to work as a television analyst for networks like ESPN, NESN, and SportsChannel. This role allowed me to witness firsthand the brilliance of some of the greatest minds in women's basketball: Pat Summitt, Andy Landers, Tara VanDerveer, C. Vivian Stringer, Bonnie Henrickson, Geno Auriemma and Chris Dailey, Jim Foster, and many more. These experiences gave me unique insight, knowledge, and voice, setting me apart as a future coach in the industry.

In addition to broadcasting, I became a basketball lecturer and co-owner of summer camps alongside my dear friend and fellow Maccabiah USA teammate, Carol. For ten years, we ran the Sherry Levin All-Star Camp and the Position Camp, which provided me with the platform to share my experiences and inspire hundreds of young basketball players. There's something truly special about seeing those young girls, sitting cross-legged on the gym floor, hanging on my every word. Their energy fueled my passion and kept me motivated to share my story.

While television production was my full-time job, I had the privilege of working as a producer behind the scenes at PrimoDonna Productions. The company had strong ties with the NBA, thanks to its president and founder, Donna Orender, another dear friend and mentor. Together, we produced one of my all-time favorite projects: *Coach to Coach: The*

Ultimate NBA Coach's Instructional Video. Legends like Pat Riley taught the Lakers' fast break, Chuck Daly shared insights on living your passion, and Rick Pitino discussed the Knicks' pressure defense. Being in the room with these basketball icons and hearing their wisdom was invaluable to my growth as a coach, particularly when it came to game management. Combining this wealth of knowledge with my experience as a broadcast analyst created a coaching perspective like no other.

Years later, after the birth of my daughter, a difficult divorce, and a return to my hometown, I found myself back in Worcester. A close friend, Cherise, who was the head coach at Worcester Polytechnic Institute, invited me to be her assistant coach. I was honored to say yes and learned so much from her. Coach Galasso gave me my shot at formalized coaching and the platform to begin with pre-game speeches. As word spread that I had returned to the area, Worcester Academy reached out to offer me the position of varsity head coach to elevate their girls' basketball program.

This marked the beginning of my twenty-four years of pre-game speeches. My coaching journey expanded to include international basketball, where I became head coach for the World Maccabiah Games, earning five gold medals. With a cumulative record of 420 wins and just ninety-seven losses, I proudly maintained an 82 percent win rate. While the record is gratifying, it's the memories, the lessons learned, and the relationships forged that will last a lifetime.

Life isn't about accumulating things. It's about creating moments—big ones, small ones, transformative ones—that shape our stories and define our journeys. When we show up in life—truly show up—with open eyes, an open heart, and an open mind, we invite these moments to find us. Moments don't just happen; they're collected like treasures, building the paths we walk and the lives we lead. This book is about that—about seeing the lessons in the moments and letting them guide us, inspire us, and teach us to live fully and authentically. After all, it's the moments that matter.

Now, you may be thinking that you are not sitting in a locker room getting ready to play a game, so why would these pre-game motivations be applicable to you? The answer lies in my belief that you can LIVE LIFE AS A PRE-GAME SPEECH. Most people's lives do not travel along a smooth road. Mine certainly did not. There are days you might feel sad, challenged, discombobulated, frustrated, and on and on, and in need of motivation. Other days, you are content, happy, and joyful. Some days, you are simply looking for inspiration to grab hold of to make it a great day.

I still send texts to my former players who now play in college: "GAMEDAY." They know the importance of that word. I believe my daily thoughts and actions are driven by my desire to share my experiences with others to teach life lessons, often based on past experiences I have had. The strands that we weave together throughout our childhood, adolescence, young adulthood, adulthood, and old age (I am getting there) create a beautiful tapestry called our story. Corny. Cheesy. Yes—I am aware. But my lens of the world creates stories that are anecdotes and lessons that can appeal to both struggles and triumphs, all wrapped up with a bow in pre-game speeches! *Pre-Game* is your playbook to get a boost of motivation.

Each of the twenty-four pre-game speeches (yes, my jersey number and lucky number) captures the essence of what I shared with my team. I'll break down how each message translated to the game, and more importantly, how you can apply those insights to living your best life. These speeches aren't meant to be a linear journey—feel free to jump around, explore, and see which one resonates with you in the moment. Whenever you need a burst of motivation, I'm confident you'll find something inspiring in any of my pre-game speeches.

Keep smiling and enjoy!

FIRST QUARTER

Authenticity Is Your Superpower

One of the first questions I ask any member of a team is: What's something we should know about you to truly understand who you are? I like this question because while it is a simple one, no one has to share more than they are comfortable with, and it allows a team to see each other with much more clarity and depth. I've had time to reflect on my own answer, after all, it's my own question. Over time, I've developed three go-to traits that represent who I am: First, I can be a bit stubborn; second, I'm a little cheesy; and third, I'm a crier.

Here's the thing: by sharing our authentic traits, we open the door to deeper connection and understanding. We're not just talking about behaviors or habits; we're showing the why behind the what. Our personalities don't come from nowhere. They're shaped by biology, upbringing, and life experiences. While they can stabilize over time, they're never set in stone. That's the beauty of it—we're always evolving, always growing, and we always have room to improve!

Growing up, my dad was both my biggest cheerleader and my toughest critic. He was the one who believed in me, no matter what I set my mind to. But he was also the one who pushed me to be better, even when it was hard to hear. And looking back, I realize how much his unconditional love and influence shaped me. One distinct memory stands out, a moment that went on to define so much of who I am today.

I was just four years old, waking up early on a Sunday morning with my sister to watch cartoons on PBS. While sitting in our den, where the one household television was, I decided to color a picture and give it to my dad when he woke up. Crayons in hand, I added colors to the black outlines of the drawing. As I scribbled the colors on the page, I was so proud of it and could hardly wait to show him. When I saw him come into the kitchen, I ran to him, holding up my drawing with a big grin, expecting a huge smile, a bear hug, and all the praise a little kid could hope for.

After my morning hug and kiss, he said, "Thank you, but I know you can do better. Your colors are outside the lines. Why don't you try again?"

Ouch. That stung. That moment stung. Hands on hips, I stormed off. My four-year-old heart was crushed. But as harsh as it was, something shifted in me—something between frustration, sadness, and determination. Maybe there were a few tears—I'm sure of it—but I wasn't going to let that be the end of it. I went back into the den, took out another picture, and concentrated on carefully staying within the lines as I colored. I came back to him with a second version. When I presented it, with a little sarcastic edge of "*Here*," his praise was exactly what I wanted to hear: "Terrific! I knew you could do it."

That moment planted a seed inside me. I applied that same determination to everything I did—school, music, sports, you name it. Whatever came my way, I gave it my all. Mostly within the lines, of course.

And then there was the time my stubbornness really showed up. Once again, my personality was shaped by experiences in my youth. My dad, a die-hard Boston sports fan, took us to all the professional sporting events—Red Sox, Patriots, Bruins, and Celtics. In those days, ticket prices were reasonable, and sometimes the arenas weren't even sold out. I loved being with my dad, not to mention the energy, the crowd, and of course, the popcorn. But what I loved more than anything was the competition. There's nothing like being a fan when each win or loss of *your team* you feel to the core.

I remember one Sunday when I was twelve, sitting at a Celtics game with my family. I was absolutely captivated. The Celtics of the 1970s were my idols—John Havlicek, Dave Cowens, JoJo White. I would practice their moves in the driveway, pretending to be them. This was long before the beginning of the WNBA. But that day, sitting during timeouts listening to the organ playing rhythmic chants, I noticed the Celtics' sneakers most of all. They were all wearing these deep, dark green shoes that weren't available to anyone in the stores. At the time, before the days of endless sneaker options, they were mostly black or white Converse and perhaps a gold or red. But these? They were green. *So cool.*

On the drive home, I proudly declared just how cool it was that the Celtics' sneakers were green. Never did I expect the swirl that would follow. My dad disagreed. "No, they were black." What? I wasn't having it. I was so confident. They were green, and there was no way anyone could convince me otherwise. The debate went on the duration of the ride home and continued in the kitchen, where my sister and mother urged me to back down. Eventually, I stormed off, my stubborn streak in full force.

With no internet to settle the argument, we had to wait until the next game to find out. The suspense was killing me. And when we got to the Boston Garden, as we walked closer and closer to the court, there they were—the sneakers were, indeed, a dark green. I was right. We all laugh about it now—the legend of the green sneakers—but my stubbornness? That's here to stay.

Then there's the cheesy side of me. I find joy in the little things—whether it's collecting good-luck charms or sharing nostalgic moments with the people I love. To this day, my daughter and I still recite "Starlight, star bright" together, and I add to my collection of good-luck charms every year. I even edit team highlight videos to Disney theme songs. Because sometimes, it's the little moments that make life a little brighter.

And of course, there's the crying. I'm not afraid to admit it—I'm a crier. Movies, TV shows, and real-life moments can get me choked up. *Glee* and *America's Got Talent* are absolute tearjerkers for me. But real-life emotional moments? Waterworks. I'll never forget my daughter's high school graduation. I was standing on stage, presenting her diploma, and I lost it the moment they started reading the long list of her accomplishments—ugly crying and all. Marcia still teases me about how I ruined the photos. But honestly, I wouldn't change a thing. It was one of the proudest moments of my life.

So, who is your authentic self? What is your superpower? Have you thought about your gifts? Who and what shaped you? Are you able to find your "aha moments" that help define who you are? In the First Quarter section of this book, you will read that being my authentic self has never been a struggle. I've always embraced who I am, flaws and all. It's not about being perfect—it's about being real.

My authenticity is my superpower. It's what helps me navigate challenges, connect with others, and stay true to who I am, even amid the most challenging times. When we show up as our true selves, something magical happens. And that, I believe, is where the real connection begins.

Each pre-game speech in this quarter tries to peel back that corner of your authentic self, to eventually reveal the unfiltered power that's been there all along—because when you stop performing and start showing up as exactly who you are, flaws and all, you tap into something no one else can replicate: your unique perspective, your specific experiences, your unrepeatable voice. Authenticity isn't just being honest—it's being your authentic self, and authenticity is your superpower.

Diamond or a Pencil

> *Everything is made of atoms. The arrangement of those atoms determines their strength, value, and purpose. Take carbon. Arrange it one way, and you get graphite: soft, fragile, the lead of a ten-cent pencil that snaps under pressure. Arrange those same carbon atoms under extreme heat and compression, and you get a diamond: rare, enduring, invaluable. Composed of the exact same building blocks, yet physically, they are very different.*
>
> *Today you have a choice. Will you play like a diamond—brilliant, resilient, forged by pressure? Or will you be the pencil—common, easily broken, quickly worn down?"*
>
> I pause, letting silence fill the space. Eye contact matters here. I lean in closer now before I continue.
>
> *The difference isn't what you're made of—it's how you choose to be shaped. Your attitude. Your mindset. Your willingness to embrace the pressure instead of breaking under it.*
>
> By now, they're nodding. Some scribble the words in their mental notebooks. Others just stare back, eyes hungry.
>
> *So choose today. Choose to play inspired. Choose to play aggressively. Choose to play smart. Choose to hustle on every single play. Choose to lift your teammates higher than yourself.*
>
> My voice drops to nearly a whisper.
>
> *A ten-cent pencil? No! Choose to be the priceless diamond.*

Choices define us. Not the big ones that come along every few years, but the thousands of small decisions we make each day. The words we speak to others. Every action we produce. Every response to adversity. These are the moments that reveal who we truly are.

That's why I begin each season with my "Diamond or the Pencil" speech. The team hears it before our first game, when possibility hangs thick in the air and every team's record still reads 0-0. It's more than just coach speak. It's the foundation of everything we build together.

These words have resonated with hundreds of players over the years, but none embodied them more completely than Alicia.

Standing 6'4", Alicia combined an imposing physical presence with fierce dedication, approaching every practice with a relentless drive to improve her game. She would eventually earn a Division I scholarship to Manhattan College. Her younger siblings eventually attended Worcester Academy too, and her parents rarely missed a game, cheering from their usual spot in the stands.

What I didn't know—what none of us knew—was the weight Alicia was carrying beneath her composed exterior.

It was 2004. We had just won our first NEPSAC Class B Championship, and the energy in Warner Auditorium was electric. We were celebrating the end of the season with a pizza party, gifts for the seniors, and the highlight video I would always edit. In typical fashion I would use Disney Songs for those uplifting moments. What I loved about highlight videos is that the opposition never scored and we never missed. Our highlight video had just finished playing on the big screen and the players and parents were beaming with pride.

As we were all saying goodbye, Alicia's mom Nancy pulled me aside, her eyes filling with tears. She started with, "I don't know if Alicia can come back to Worcester next year." Words that I never anticipated hearing after such a stellar freshman season and growth. Her next words were like a dagger.

"Ed has ALS," she whispered.

The world seemed to stop. Ed—Alicia's father. The gentle giant who always thanked me after games. The man whose pride in his daughter radiated without saying a word. Ed has amyotrophic lateral sclerosis (ALS)?

"We don't know if Alicia can return next year," Nancy reiterated.

I squeezed her hand. "We'll find a way." We hugged.

And we did. Through the generosity of the Worcester Academy George B. Berg Family Scholarship, Alicia returned. But she didn't just show up—she transformed.

Every day she walked into that gym with grace, with grit, with steely resolve. Never complained. Never made excuses. Never let her teammates see the weight she was carrying. She practiced harder. Competed fiercer. Embraced every challenge as if it were a gift rather than a burden.

And Ed—he showed up too. At an away game at Kingswood Oxford in Connecticut, I went down the hall and down the stairs to get a bottle of water from a vending machine. Ed was entering the building and we greeted each other with usual pleasantries. I started to run back quickly to watch warm-ups, and I'll never forget what I saw when I turned around. Ed was slowly climbing the stairs, cane in hand, each step a deliberate act of love. "I'll just take my time," he said with a quiet dignity.

Ten years later, when I went through my own cancer treatment, those words came back to me. I finally understood what that kind of perseverance truly meant.

That same week, Alicia marked a career-high in points then broke her own record the very next game. She wasn't just finding her rhythm on the court. She was choosing—daily, hourly—to be the diamond.

In 2006, we captured the NEPSAC Class A Championship with an undefeated season. In the celebration-filled locker room afterward, Alicia walked in clutching a basketball and a Sharpie. "Could everyone sign this?" she asked. "It's for my dad."

Ed was waiting on the court, now wheelchair-bound and unable to speak. We gathered around him, our victory shouts replaced by silent tears, as we placed the signed ball in his lap. His eyes said everything words couldn't. He knew what his daughter had accomplished. He understood the heart behind her triumph.

Ed passed away that August, just before Alicia's senior year.

But true diamonds don't lose their luster when the light dims. Alicia thrived at Manhattan College, then came home to become a teacher and later, my assistant coach at Worcester Academy. In 2022, I attended her wedding at Aldrich Mansion in Rhode Island. The forecast had promised perfect weather and breathtaking ocean views. Instead, rain poured and thick fog erased the horizon completely.

The ceremony was a beautiful and emotional affair. I was so grateful to share in her special day. As I hugged her goodbye, Alicia whispered, "Coach, I wouldn't have gotten through today without all you taught me. I woke up to a cold, rainy day—but I chose to embrace the joy."

That's what the diamond looks like!

Driving home from her wedding, I felt that rare, complete satisfaction that reminds me why I coach. It's never been about championship banners or win-loss records. It's about these moments—witnessing young women like Alicia become resilient, gracious, grounded leaders long after the final whistle blows.

The "Diamond or the Pencil" isn't just a pre-game speech. It's a daily decision we all face. When life applies pressure—and it will—you have a choice. You can crumble like graphite, point fingers, make excuses. Or you can harness that pressure to become something extraordinary.

Be mindful. Be present. Be intentional.

And when life squeezes hardest, remember: Diamonds are just carbon that refuses to break.

Choose to be the diamond. Every single time.

212 Degrees

"At 211 degrees, water is hot. At 212 degrees, it boils. And with boiling water comes steam. And steam can power a train."

—Sam Parker

One extra degree makes all the difference.

That 'extra degree' captures the essence of excellence in the most memorable way.

One more action is all it takes—one more pass, one more drive, one more free throw, one more rebound, one more defensive stop.

Just one more.

If everyone commits to giving just a little extra, we become stronger and more powerful together.

It's that one extra degree that separates good from great.

I love this metaphor because it captures a simple truth: One degree more can change everything. That one extra push—when you think you've already given all you have—is what transforms effort into power, and potential into momentum.

I shared this lesson with my team one late-season game. Fatigue had set in. Bodies were sore, confidence was shaky, and distractions were everywhere. Before tip-off, I reminded them: "We're already hot. But what would it take to be boiling? What's the extra degree you can give tonight— for yourself, and for the team?"

And then it happened. One of our smallest guards, nearly spent, dove flat-out on the hardwood for a loose ball. She came up with it, threw it to a teammate, and we scored. That single play turned the energy of the game.

The bench erupted, the crowd roared, and I could see in my players' eyes that they understood: It wasn't about the scoreboard yet—it was about the willingness to give that extra degree.

That willingness has shaped me since my own high school days.

Back then, I was a three-sport athlete. Soccer came first in the fall, followed by basketball and then track and field. Unfortunately, the physical and emotional toll from the soccer coach drained me season after season. By junior year, after a crushing loss in the state semi-finals, I knew I couldn't keep pouring myself into something that left me burned out before basketball even began. So I walked away from soccer my senior year and made a commitment: my "one degree more" would be basketball.

One afternoon, I was playing in our school's simulated outdoor area (SOA), a big space with courts, an indoor track, and gymnastics equipment. I was the only girl in the game, competing with and against the boys who would be on the varsity basketball team. I knew that this was the best way to sharpen my skills.

During one of those pickup runs, I noticed the athletic director standing in the doorway. I wanted to prove that I could hold my own and show off my skills. My defensive stance got a little lower, my talking became louder, and my intensity skyrocketed.

The other team missed a shot, and my teammate grabbed the rebound. I took off in transition—sprinting. Just one more degree, which for me in that moment meant one step faster, I told myself. I crossed halfcourt at full speed, reaching the free throw line just as the ball sailed toward me, over the outstretched hands of a defender. It was barely out of reach.

Still sprinting, I suddenly realized: I was out of court.

The cinder block wall loomed five feet away. Instinctively, I crouched to avoid going face-first and slammed into the ventilation grate. The side of my head, my right elbow—fifteen stitches in both. A bloody mess. But that instinct—to give it everything, to literally run through a wall for the ball—became a defining trait. I don't recommend literally doing that, but metaphorically? Absolutely. Find the one thing that drives you toward your better self.

The lesson extends far beyond sports. In the workforce, not every day is going to feel fulfilling. Some days are a grind. But if you can find just one thing to do a little better—one task you finish well, one kind word you offer, one gesture of gratitude—you shift your outlook. That extra degree makes a difference.

And imagine if everyone committed to one more act of kindness, one more encouraging word, one more small effort beyond what's required. It wouldn't just change teams or workplaces. It would change the world.

Changing just one habit can be enough to shift everything. Something as simple as putting your phone away at dinner. Or trying not to check emails after a certain hour. Think of ways to incorporate one thing each day in your routine rather than completely alter your life. One thing seems so much more attainable.

Pay it forward—with just one more degree.

So I ask you: Where in your life are you sitting at 211 degrees? And what would it mean to push yourself—just a little more—to 212.

Pebble in the Water

> *What happens when you drop a pebble into a pool of water? Close your eyes and envision it. The one tiny pebble dropped in the water creates ripples. First, small ripples immediately around the spot of impact, then larger and larger ones as they move away from the center.*
>
> *One pebble, hitting the water, can create waves that extend further and further.*
>
> *Be the pebble that sparks others. That makes others better around you. And be the person who takes responsibility for creating the energy source of positivity and success. Help your teammates when they're down or make a mistake.*
>
> *Your actions speak louder than words. Positivity is contagious. Be the one who starts the ripple.*

I have a poster in my office that says: "Attitude: A little thing that makes a BIG difference." Behind the words is an image of ripples across water. I love this visual because it symbolizes how much impact one person can have. Your energy is contagious. It can inspire and influence others in ways you might not even realize.

The ability to visualize is an essential tool, especially for athletes. When I consult with individual athletes or teams about building leadership skills and building mental toughness, I often talk about visualization as a skill to reduce stress and build mental toughness. Imagine it. Picture it. Rehearse it in your mind. Then, when you're actually in that situation, your brain knows how to respond.

That's why this "Pebble in the Water" speech became one of my early go-to messages for teams when they were still forming. From day one,

I wanted them to understand: success is never about just one person. It takes every member, and even small actions—a rebound, a word of encouragement, a hustle play—can shift an entire outcome. Making the people around you better is the ultimate measure of leadership.

What energy do you bring to the room? Are you an energy vampire? Energy vampires are people who—sometimes unintentionally—drain your emotional energy. They feed on your willingness to listen and care for them, leaving you exhausted and overwhelmed. Energy vampires can be anywhere and anyone. The only way to defeat them is to stop them in their tracks.

The hardest thing to do is to stop the negative action before it becomes a chain reaction. We've all been there—one negative thought brings you down the rabbit hole of creating more negative thoughts. Before you know it, what your boss said, what your friend did, can bring you down. The idea of visualizing the pebble is to understand that this is a ripple effect that can be changed. You have the mental capacity to step back and change the action. Turn the situation into a positive perspective or at least neutralize your negativity. Every interaction we have, no matter how small, has the potential to create a ripple effect. When we positively influence someone, they may, in turn, influence others, creating a chain reaction of positive change. Similarly, negative influences can propagate destructive patterns—those energy vampires.

Find the good in something and see how that becomes the positive ripple effect. More and more goodwill surely follows.

So, I'll admit, I'm a bit of a fan. It's not often that someone captures my attention like this, but when I met Dr. Olenda Johnson, I was instantly hooked. Through Donna Orender's network and Generation W, I've had the privilege of connecting with extraordinary women from all walks of life. In 2017, I had the responsibility of being the stage manager for Generation W's signature event, which focused on the theme "Imagination, Innovation, Inspiration." Dr. Olenda was a featured mainstage speaker.

Our introduction was brief, in the green room, where speakers gather before or after their presentations. But within moments, I felt like I was meeting a rock star. Olenda's warmth, grace, positivity, and sheer joy were magnetic. As it happened, her parents were there too, proudly watching her speak in person for the first time. They were equally poised and beaming with pride.

My role as stage manager was multidimensional. First, I had to ensure each speaker made it from the green room to the stage on time. I coordinated with the audio team to make sure microphones were ready, whether handheld or wireless headset. But beyond logistics, part of my job was to help speakers feel at ease. Backstage, we kept our voices low, offering quiet support before they stepped into the spotlight.

Olenda was understandably nervous as this was her first mainstage presentation in front of 1,300 people. We chatted a bit about our New England connections, I gave her a few words of encouragement, and stepped back allowing her to focus on what would be a truly remarkable speech that earned a rousing standing ovation.

When she came offstage, we shared a hug—a transformational moment that I'll never forget. The energy of her adrenaline and nerves had transformed into pure joy as she took the stage and left an indelible impact on everyone in the room with her inspiring words. Years later, Olenda shared that our hug was "something that just changed everything," and in that unexpected moment, we both recognized how something small can become profoundly transformative.

With that hug, in that shared experience, we both found something unexpected and beautiful—the kind of connection that ripples out in ways we couldn't have predicted.

Her mainstage presentation was so powerful and impactful that I felt compelled to share her wisdom with my basketball team. True to Olenda's generous spirit, she visited Worcester Academy to meet with us and speak to the girls about leadership. I still remember the main points she left us with: First, always give your best. And second, "don't make someone else's issue your issue." Great advice not only for high school girls, but for everyone! That conversation was like a pebble creating ripples—ultimately contributing to our victory in the NEPSAC Class AA Championship.

Dr. Olenda is a familiar and cherished presence at Generation W events. Her radiant energy never fails to illuminate the room, leaving everyone uplifted and inspired... especially me, her #1 fan.

Head, Guts, Heart

To achieve greatness in anything, you need three essential elements: your head, your guts, and your heart.

Your head gives you focus and intelligence. Your guts give you courage and determination. Your heart gives you passion and perseverance. Bring all three to every challenge, and you will find a way through.

Think about the big moments in your life—the joys and the obstacles. Think about how you navigate them. Think about your head, guts, and heart.

This philosophy I found on the track. As a high school sprinter, I learned early that every race is won or lost in those three places: head, guts, and heart.

I can still feel the tension mounting as I readied my body at the starting line. My heart was pounding. "On your mark," the starter called. I lowered myself into the blocks, coiled and ready. My good-luck charms swung around my neck like a pendulum, keeping time. "Set." I rose, perfectly still except for the adrenaline surging through my veins. Then—"Bang!" The starter's gun.

That first explosion out of the blocks was the head. Sprinting is technical. The start is rehearsed a hundred times in practice: proper angle, quick reaction, perfect drive. If you master the mechanics, you gain a crucial edge in those first ten meters.

The middle of the race—that long stretch where your lungs burn and your legs churn in rhythm with barely a thought —is all guts. It's the sheer speed you've trained for, combined with whatever gifts are in your DNA.

It's the majority of the race, and there's nowhere to hide. Just you, your breath, and your willpower.

And the final ten meters? That's pure heart. When your body is screaming to stop, when your legs feel like cement, it's your heart that propels you forward. That last ounce of will, that refusal to give in, is what carries you across the finish line.

I ended many of my pre-game speeches the same way: *All three today. Head. Guts. Heart. That's what brings us to victory.*

Years later, I would need that same mantra off the track, when life gave me the race I never wanted to run.

I was one of those women who never lingered in the waiting room for the results of my mammogram. Always on the go, and with no history of breast cancer in my family, I'd check the box that said, "Mail me my results." But on June 26, 2014, something changed. This time, hours after my exam, I received a call from the radiologist, asking me to schedule a biopsy as soon as possible because something suspicious had shown up on the 3D scans. I didn't panic. It's probably nothing. Benign, I thought. I didn't even tell anyone. Why would I make them worry for nothing?

That evening, my daughter Marcia and I were attending a Billy Joel concert at Fenway Park. Seeing Billy Joel perform was a long-awaited item on my bucket list. But even as I enjoyed the music, singing loudly the songs of my teen years, the scheduled biopsy was on my mind.

The next day, I had the biopsy. I still didn't tell anyone, not even my daughter. It will be a false alarm, I was sure of it. Benign.

This was my first breast biopsy, so I didn't know exactly what to expect. I was briefed on the procedure: The radiologist would take a needle biopsy of the mass and insert a metal clip in the spot. When I asked the nurse about the clip, she told me, "It will remain in your body for as long as you live, or if you have cancer, the surgeon will use it to locate the cancer." That was an unexpected piece of information for sure. The radiologist said they would call with the results in a few days.

Yes, it hurts! The nurse suggested taking pain medication and resting, but I wondered, does going to a sold-out Zac Brown Band concert again at Fenway Park count as resting? Dancing, singing, and keeping my left arm tucked in to protect the biopsy site was challenging, but I managed. In my mind, this would just be a scare, and the results would be benign. This is not part of my story. Or was it?

The third of July arrived, and the radiologist told me that he would call at a certain time. Marcia and I had just finished the school year and we were enjoying the beginning of summer break. We were both hanging out at home, so I told her I was going to fill the car with gas. I took the call in the car and parked down the street. The accent of the radiologist's voice still is heard in my head. He said, "I'm sorry to tell you, you have breast cancer."

My mind went blank. *No. Not me. This can't be my story. My daughter's about to be a senior in high school. What???*

The radiologist's calm, monotone voice continued, telling me it was stage 1, caught early, and I'd need to decide on a course of treatment.

I sat in my car, stunned. Moments after my tears and shock, something inside shifted. I needed to fight. My head told me to gather information, to find the best doctors and a strategy. My guts told me to step into the fire and face it. My heart reminded me who I was fighting for—Marcia, and for myself.

My shock, sadness, and fear gradually gave way to a quiet, insistent question: *Now what?* I reached for my phone and called my dear friend Marianne. The words sat heavy in my throat, reluctant to be spoken, until I finally managed to whisper them into existence: "I have breast cancer."

She stayed on the phone. We talked a bit. I cried a bit. Then, almost immediately, something shifted—I had to fight. I focused on finding the best doctors, the right treatment, and building a support network. This wasn't the end of my story. It was just the beginning of the fight to live.

Telling Marcia was one of the hardest moments of my life. I walked into the living room, where she sat watching TV, and said, "I have some good news and some bad news. The good news is I will be fine. The bad news is, I have breast cancer." We cried, we hugged, and we promised to face it together.

From that moment on, it was a race. My general doctor, oncologist, and my medical team at Dana-Farber became my coaches, my guides, and my support. They gave me options, strategies, and encouragement.

I ultimately found myself on the edge of a big decision: endure the grueling chemo and radiation, hoping to lower the chances of recurrence, or skip chemo and go straight to radiation. I also wanted to schedule the treatments around my game schedule. After each report came back, they analyzed my cancer and presented me with options. Each time my oncologist would ask, "What do you want to do?" My answer, tinged with sarcasm, was always, "You're the professional, you tell me." More genetic tests would be taken and more decisions to be made. Marianne would attend every doctor's appointment with me, God bless her, and take copious notes. My mind would be a jumbled mess filled with what-ifs and what-nows.

While nearing the end of the decision process, I'll never forget the weighted words from my oncologist who said, "Your decision will be based on your personality. If my mother and mother-in-law had the same diagnosis, they would choose opposite treatments." With that perspective, I made my decision: I would do whatever it took. *Head, Guts, Heart.* After the Mass General Hospital Tumor Board reviewed my case and recommended chemo, I was ALL IN. Two days later, I had my first of four debilitating and agonizing chemo treatments.

On July 21, I had surgery. Everything went smoothly, and the cancer was removed with "clear margins." This meant no cancerous cells were found at the edges of the tissue taken out, a sign that all visible cancer had been successfully removed, greatly reducing the chance of recurrence. Thank God.

By the first week of August, my basketball team was registered for our annual summer tournament at Assumption College. It was a great opportunity for the girls to bond while staying overnight at a hotel and competing. I was advised not to drive the van, so I asked my assistant coach to handle it. That night, while at the hotel, I gathered the girls together to share the news. We were playing games and all laughing in my room. It was the perfect time to tell them. When I did, they went silent, eyes wide in shock. They were high school girls after all, without a clue of how to process this information. Some cried. Some teared up. I quickly reassured them, "I will be fine. I will still be your coach. But I will need your help."

As each player left my room, they all lined up for a hug. Perhaps a reassurance that they cared and that we are in this together.

The pain and suffering from the treatments sometimes felt unbearable. I wanted to quit. There were moments when I genuinely didn't think I could go on. It was that bad. But my guts kept me going. With Marcia's incredible support, I marked each day off my calendar with a red Sharpie, counting down the days. She was my rock. Each night, she would climb into bed with me while I rested, and she would do her homework. I would essentially collapse after a long day at work and practice. One more red X was one day closer to health.

Those in "the know" would bring food for not just me, but also Marcia. Those in "the know" would send care packages and cards. Those in "the know" showed up every day with a word of encouragement. Chemo treatments are cumulative. By the second one, I was just hanging on. A trip to the emergency room, losing my voice, and pain in every inch of my body left me wondering if I could withstand the final two treatments. Marcia looked at me and said, "Mom, you are halfway through. Only two more. You cannot quit now. You can do it." Words spoken like a true coach!

She was right. What was the alternative? There was none. When life gets tough, you find a way through. You use your head and your guts. The quote, "When going through hell… keep going," couldn't have been more fitting.

My guts also meant I didn't want to share my struggle with others. People close to me knew. But there were times while wearing my wig, when a colleague would compliment my hair, saying, "It looks so nice today." Depending on my mood, I might respond with a sarcastic grin, "It'll look like this tomorrow." Some days, it took me twenty minutes to walk from my athletic director's office to the second floor because I had to stop halfway to catch my breath. One step at a time. Then rest.

The chemo was crushing, and each time, I lost my voice. Imagine a coach without a voice? But somehow, the girls seemed to understand me better when I couldn't speak. They had to focus on my facial expressions, hand signals, and paper signs. My assistant coach, Caleigh, a former Worcester Academy player, was a godsend. She drove me when I couldn't drive and yelled out the instructions I whispered to her. Normally, I walked the sidelines during games, in heels, even. But during treatment, I traded my heels for flats. Despite everything, the girls did their part, and we won the conference banner for the third consecutive season.

Then there was the heart. I wanted so much to be there for Marcia; to help her with her college essays, go on college campus visits, and celebrate her momentous accomplishments. I was determined to be at her cum laude recognition ceremony, and I was! My heart beamed with pride, not only for her academic prowess but also knowing that she put her fears aside to help me.

Through this defining chapter of my life, I learned not only about myself but also about the people I surround myself with. I discovered who my true, supportive friends were. My heart helped me understand what truly matters in life and what we can shrug off as insignificant.

Marcia would be accepted to the prestigious Johns Hopkins University and be recognized for five senior awards in high school. She shone not only for herself but also for giving me strength when I needed it most.

When you're standing at a crossroads, uncertain which path to take, you might turn to a friend and ask, "What do you think I should do?" The answers often come wrapped in familiar wisdom: "Follow your heart," or "Trust your gut." But sometimes, a quieter voice whispers, "Follow your head."

The truth is, the wisest decisions aren't made by choosing one over the others—they're made by honoring all three. Your heart speaks the language of your deepest values and what truly matters to you. Your gut carries the wisdom of instinct, that inexplicable knowing that comes from somewhere beyond words. And your head offers clarity, reason, and the ability to see the bigger picture.

When you learn to listen to all three—really listen—they become a chorus guiding you toward what's right for this moment, for *your* moment. And once you've made your choice, GO ALL IN!. Let your head chart the course with focus and intention. Let your gut give you the strength to push through when the path gets steep. And let your heart be your constant companion, sustaining you with purpose.

Shamash Candle

In every menorah, one candle sits higher than the others. It's the shamash—the helper candle. Its job is to light all the others, one by one.

Without the shamash, the menorah remains dark. With it, the light spreads, multiplying until the whole menorah glows.

The shamash doesn't shine for itself. Its purpose is to ignite the flame in others. To serve. To lead by lifting others up. That's what I ask of you today: Be the shamash. Be the one who lights the way for your teammates. Be the one who makes everyone around you shine. The shamash does not lose any of its own brightness by making others bright.

I love this message because it weaves together a cherished tradition from my Jewish faith with a universal lesson for everyone. For the team, the takeaway is simple: Team success happens when individuals support one another and shine together.

Jealousy and envy, unfortunately, surface in all stages of life—from childhood to adulthood. One of the highest compliments a person can receive is that they make those around them better. Surrounding yourself with positive people who lift you up, without fearing they'll lose something in the process, is essential for growth and success.

When I was an athletic director, I made it a priority to uplift all programs equally, not just the girls' basketball team. While coaching basketball was my primary role, I was intentional about celebrating the achievements of the soccer teams and the golf, tennis, and fencing squads with the same enthusiasm. The lesson was clear: Recognizing others' success does not diminish your own. In fact, it creates a culture of mutual respect and shared accomplishment.

Celebrating others' victories doesn't diminish your own light—it actually makes it shine brighter. When you genuinely appreciate someone else's achievements while working on becoming your best self, magic happens. These aren't competing forces pulling you in different directions; they're dance partners, lifting each other in perfect harmony.

I know, I know—easier said than done. But isn't that true for most things worth doing?

There's an important distinction I emphasize between a player's *role* and their *value* to the team—a concept that applies just as much in business as it does in sports. Simply put, a role is *what you do*, while value is *what you bring*. For example, in basketball, a role might be the leading scorer, the most accurate three-point shooter, or the best rebounder. But a player's value goes beyond their stats; it could be their ability to uplift teammates, inject humor when the team needs a laugh, or even something as simple yet impactful as being quick with a water bottle during a critical timeout. Everyone has value to offer.

The key is to embrace your unique value. As my dad always said, "Put blinders on." What that means is focus on yourself, not others. Lean into your strengths, trust in your abilities, and believe in your own superpower. By doing so, you'll not only maximize your contribution but also inspire those around you to do the same.

Sharing your authentic self with your team, organization, workplace, or family is the most valuable gift you can offer because it's—*you*. No one else can bring your unique perspective, talents, and essence to the world. Embrace your qualities and share them with those around you. Are you the one who finds humor in the face of adversity? The pragmatic thinker who navigates tough decisions with clarity? The warm presence that comforts during times of sadness? The grateful person who finds joy in the everyday? These traits are just a glimpse of the extraordinary power that lies in being authentic. Believe in your superpower—it's what makes you irreplaceable.

In my first year coaching at Worcester Academy in 2001, we traveled to The Williston School for our final game before winter break. It was a long bus ride, and I could sense the weariness in the team. Finals had drained them, and thoughts of the holidays were already pulling their focus. It was also one of the eight nights of Hanukkah, and lighting the candles was on my mind. Many of my pre-game speeches took shape during my thirty-five-minute commute to Worcester, and this one came together on that journey.

In the away locker room, I shared my pre-game speech. As the only Jewish person in the room, I explained the significance of the shamash candle, the helper candle that lights the others, allowing them to shine. The room fell silent, and the team was captivated. Their energy soon shifted, and their buy-in was palpable. We were ready to face a formidable and talented opponent.

What I didn't realize was how prophetic my words would be. Late in the first half, Charde, our star player, went down with a severe ankle sprain. At halftime, I reminded them that they all needed to shine. That not one person could replace Charde's talent and contributions, but each player needed to add a little more to make us all shine. As Charde cheered us on while sitting on the bench with an ice pack wrapped around her foot, the team had to step up and carry the load without her. And step up they did. Each player glowed in her own way, and together, they outperformed a talented Williston squad.

We won on the scoreboard that day, but the real victory was the team's realization that they all had the power to contribute without dimming their own light. They didn't just win the game—they discovered the strength of unity and the brilliance of stepping up when it matters most.

So, the next time you step into your arena and onto your proverbial court, ask yourself: *Am I the shamash today? Am I lifting others? Am I helping the light spread?*

Be the shamash. Light the way.

Stronger Together

I hold up a single blank tongue depressor.

This tongue depressor represents the individual player who only cares about herself. She's selfish on the court and off. She thinks she can do it all alone. That player is easily broken.

I snap the tongue depressor in half with ease and set it aside.

See? Broken. Done. Game over. Now, watch this.

I gather all the personalized tongue depressors into a stack, holding them firmly with both hands.

These represent our team. A team that's unselfish. A team that supports each other, works hard to be the best version of themselves, and understands that we are much, much stronger together. This cannot be easily broken.

I attempt with all my strength to break the stack—it remains intact, barely bending.

I'm trying with everything I have, and I can't break it. The stack of tongue depressors remains intact. Unbreakable.

That's us. That's what we are when we choose to be stronger together. Every single one of your sticks matters. Every single one of you matters. When we support each other, when we play for something bigger than ourselves, when we remember that our individual success is tied to our collective success—we become unbreakable.

So, I want you to remember this moment. When you're tired, when someone's getting more minutes than you think they deserve, when you're frustrated—remember these tongue depressors. Remember that you have a choice. You can be that single stick, easily broken. Or you can be part of something unbreakable. You can be part of something special.

Which will you choose?

The idea that we are stronger together is a timeless truth that resonates across both sports and life. It is a principle that underscores the power of collaboration, unity, and mutual support, showing how individuals can achieve greater heights by working collectively rather than in isolation.

In team sports, teamwork is the backbone of success. Whether on the basketball court or in rowing, no single player can achieve victory alone. Collaboration allows teammates to leverage each other's strengths, compensate for weaknesses, and develop strategies that are greater than the sum of their parts. Some games will be better than others, but it takes many to have great success.

As an English major at Holy Cross, I read a 1940 Thomas Wolfe novel that included the sentence, "You can never go home again." This sentence is meant to infer how nostalgia causes us to view the past in an overly positive light, and how humans tend to remember people and places from our upbringing in static terms. That theme, for some reason, always stuck with me. In 2016, when I got the call from then Worcester Academy's athletic director asking if I would return to be the head coach of its girls varsity basketball, I felt like I was in fact "going home."

I remember the conversation as if it were yesterday. I was working as the stage manager at Generation W's signature thought leadership event in Jacksonville, Florida. I saw on my phone that the head of the school was calling me. *Ooh, what could this call be about?* Unfortunately, I had to immediately let his call go to voicemail and listen to the message during my break. The message was brief. He and the athletic director asked me to call them back as soon as possible. So, I did. They said that the current girls' head coach was leaving, and would I come back?

Let me digress for some background context. I joined the Worcester Academy community in 2001. The head of the school at the time was masterful at recognizing people's values and finding opportunities for them. For example, based on all the experiences on my resume, he created the events coordinator position in the Alumni and Development Office for me. I ended up taking over a program that had great potential with a strong junior class. In my first three years, we went to the NEPSAC Class B Championship games, finally winning it in 2004—the first NEPSAC

Championship in Worcester Academy girls basketball history. After that win, our program went up to Class A and was undefeated in 2006, winning our second championship. I had helped established one of the top programs in New England and continued to attract some of the most talented players.

In the spring of 2008, I was pursued by a local private school to be their athletic director and girls' varsity basketball coach which I left in 2015 after my daughter graduated and after I endured breast cancer treatments. The timing now to return was perfect.

Back to the phone call. Without hesitation, I said, "YES!"

Now that you're caught up, a few weeks later, I sat in the athletic director's office going over the details. Ed Reilly and then assistant athletic director, Julie Berberian, handed me a roster and suggested that I might want to reach out to one of the girls' basketball players, Aliyah Boston, and her parents. The first thing I did when I got home was reach out to Aliyah's mom, Cleone. We spoke for ninety minutes. Cleone is one of the most sincere, spiritual, and quality people I have met. I spoke to her from the heart—my authentic self—rather than trying to sell her on having Aliyah stay at Worcester Academy. After watching all of the videos of Aliyah's freshman year, I was confident enough to say, "Aliyah could be one of the best women's basketball players of all time. Not just in high school, but eventually in the WNBA." I recognized through my experienced lens of working as a television broadcast analyst with the best coaches and high-level players that Aliyah's skill set was extraordinary. I asked Cleone to put her faith in me to guide and teach Aliyah not only about basketball but also about life lessons. Thankfully, all worked out, and they put their faith in me as a coach.

My next call was to my former player, Alicia, who recently graduated from Manhattan College. She was a teacher in the area, and I loved her as a person. Alicia was 6'4, so my wanting her as my valuable assistant coach was twofold. I knew that one of the challenges would be making a player of Aliyah's stature and skill set improve in practice. I mean, how many prep programs actually have two talented players over six feet tall? Thank goodness, Alicia joined us and worked against Aliyah in practice. This allowed me to focus on coaching Aliyah to where I thought she would go, not to where she was. I used to say, "You can do that now, but when you're against the 6'6 pro, you will need to do that better."

Championship Sunday in 2018 was an example of this mentality. To get to the championship game, we had to beat a rival, Northfield Mount Hermon (NMH). They had a talented group of players who eventually earned D1 scholarships. We hosted them at Worcester Academy, which made a huge difference to have a gym full of screaming students all cheering for us. The game was close until the end, when Aliyah blocked a shot taken by their 6'2 player and then drove the length of the court to make the layup that sealed our victory. Ahh, yes, so many hours of ball handling and guard workouts paid off. As we were celebrating our victory and chanting, "We're going to the 'ship, yeah! We're going to the 'ship, yeah," Our trainer came over to me and whispered Molly had a concussion and was in the training room.

My heart sank to my stomach. Molly was one of our valuable starters, a major contributor to our success, and an all-around wonderful person who always put the team first. I rushed to the training room to find Molly lying on the training table. Her face was soaked with tears. We hugged, and I said everything would be okay. The team soon followed me into the training room, and then her dad came in. The next thing I knew, the entire team was crying with Molly. I think in part because of Molly's heartbreak over not being able to play in the championship, but also for themselves. How could we possibly replace Molly?

At that moment, I knew that despite crying on the inside, I had to be strong for the girls. I had to present confidence that they would not see through. I led them into the locker room and said, "We all feel heartache for Molly, but we have a game to play. Erianna, you will start, and we will be fine. You will be great!" Erianna was a freshman who was filled with raw potential, and athleticism. I knew it was a tall task, but we had a young team with not much depth.

The next morning, we met for an on-court walk-through, lunch, and the bus ride to the host site at Nobles and Greenough School to face perennial power and rival, Tabor Academy. Tabor was coached by a friend of mine, Will Becker, who I had great respect for as a coach, and who I battled for a run at the championship before. Now, here I was again, in a back-and-forth battle with a talented team. They had two players over 6'3 who would attend D1 programs, as well as scholarship-level guards. But they were no match for Aliyah's skills, and the only way to slow her down was to get her in foul trouble. And that is what they did. Aliyah got in early foul trouble, but with such a young team, I knew that I could not take her out. Other players, Adara for one, a junior guard, hit some crucial three-pointers, and we built a six-point lead at halftime. Aliyah was battling double-team defense and aggressive play with her three personal fouls.

I told Aliyah at halftime to play cautiously on defense. Not soft, but cautious. Not to block shots, but to keep her arms straight up and try to disrupt their shots. The last sixteen-minute half began, and with just under twelve minutes to play, Aliyah got her fourth foul. At that point, the collective sigh from the Worcester fan base was palpable. The packed bleachers of students went silent. I took Aliyah out and had to substitute another freshman, Callie, who only played sparingly during the season.

My game management experience and understanding of Aliyah's competitive drive were what determined my next move. I walked down the bench to Aliyah, who was obviously emotional. Her fire to win was bright, and sitting on the bench was not in her DNA. I leaned in so that only she would hear me. I said, "Aliyah, you have two choices: You can sit on the bench and be sad, or you can go in now and play with four fouls until the game ends, or you foul out." I knew that if I waited to put Aliyah back in with six minutes or so left in the game, which is what most textbook coaches would do, we would most likely be down and not able to recover. But I had confidence in Aliyah. Not only is she a fierce competitor, but a perfectionist. Her basketball IQ would allow her to do everything in her power to stay in the game.

When I later watched the recording of the game, the announcers were incredulous that I put her back in. But they didn't know my team, they didn't know Aliyah, and they didn't know me. The game would go down to the final minute, where we would survive to win, and Aliyah would be named most valuable player (MVP) of the tournament. Molly sat on the bench, cheering us on. Adara was the scoring leader, hitting six threes. Kiera, one of our toughest competitors and skilled players, was not only tough on defense but she contributed leadership. Erianna gave us incredible quality minutes. And 5'4 guard Livi hit a ten-foot runner to seal the victory. Everyone contributed to a memorable effort and a lesson in being stronger together.

During it all, I was demanding, never demeaning. I pushed my players to the depths of what I thought they could do. But there were times that I realized having fun was just as important to our success as sprinting at the end of every practice.

True to that promise, we returned stronger and more determined, capturing back-to-back NEPSAC AA Championships. And Aliyah emerged as our cornerstone. With Aliyah's parents in Saint Thomas of the US Virgin Islands, I stayed closely connected with her mother, Cleone. I would call her after games and keep her updated whenever there was news.

Ultimately, Aliyah chose to attend the University of South Carolina to play for the legendary Hall of Fame coach Dawn Staley, a decision that thrilled everyone invested in her success. Ironically, many of the coaches recruiting Aliyah were players I had once announced as a sports broadcaster during their own college careers, including Dawn Staley when she played at the University of Virginia.

The old gym at Worcester Academy, with its vintage charm reminiscent of the iconic gym in the movie *Hoosiers*, became the hub of excitement during Aliyah's junior year. On open gym days, it was packed with college coaches eager to see her talent firsthand. I would meticulously arrange chairs, place cold water bottles, and chat with the coaches while pickup games unfolded—a surreal yet gratifying experience, knowing we were witnessing the start of something truly special.

The funny thing is that other college coaches could not speak with Aliyah due to National Collegiate Athletic Association (NCAA) rules; they could only speak with me. And they really didn't watch the action—after all, it was not really organized basketball, and Aliyah would completely dominate. What they wanted was for Aliyah to know that they were there.

I, on the other hand, wanted them to know that Aliyah was a good person, who worked hard, and they would be crazy not to recruit her. To Aliyah's credit and her upbringing, she didn't let all the attention go to her head. She was taught by her parents to be humble and appreciative of all she had.

I'll never forget when at the end of her sophomore year, I received an email that said: "Congratulations, Coach! Your Player is the Massachusetts Gatorade Player of the Year," I immediately teared up and called Cleone. It was early in the morning, but I couldn't wait. We both cried. Then we woke Aliyah up to tell her the news. These are the moments and the reason I coach.

Aliyah went on to win a national championship with South Carolina and earn SEC Freshman of the Year honors. She captured the Lisa Leslie Award as the nation's top center for four consecutive years—an unprecedented feat—while becoming a four-time All-American; just to name a few of her well deserved honors. Upon graduation, she was selected as the number one overall pick in the WNBA draft.

That is the legacy of stronger together.

Families, workplaces, friendships, and communities thrive on it too. Unity multiplies strength. Support ignites resilience. When you choose to put the group above yourself, you become unbreakable.

So, when you face the moments that challenge you and test your spirit, ask yourself: Will you be the single stick, or will you be part of the unbreakable stack?

Choose to be stronger together.

SECOND QUARTER

Take Action

My soccer cleats click-clacked down the cement floor of the girls' locker room as I was picking up my clarinet and books out of my locker. Tears blurred my vision—not from the sting of defeat, but from the overwhelming feeling of triumph. We had just claimed the Junior High School Newton City Championship, but the victory for me felt different. I could hear the boys hollering through the walls of the locker room. You see it wasn't simply a win. It was the culmination of a journey that had stretched beyond the field and into the very core of who I was. My desire to compete at the highest level, to push the boundaries of what was expected of me, had led me to a place few girls had ventured: the boy's varsity soccer team.

It wasn't just about skill or strength. It was about defying the norms and pushing past limitations. My competitive spirit often eclipsed the social dynamics of team sports, which in many ways made my journey even lonelier. I didn't intend to break the norms and yet, there I was, standing as a testament to what resilience and determination could achieve. I was the leading goal scorer; not the most skilled player but in my position, scoring goals was my role. How I got there was an accumulation of decisions made along the way.

In the early days of Title IX legislation, when the playing field for female athletes was still unlevel, my choice to compete with boys was yet again something supported by my parents. I had proven something to myself—that my strength could break through walls, that my resilience could redefine what it meant to be an athlete.

I was in fourth grade in 1972, the year that President Richard M. Nixon signed Title IX, a federal law that prohibits sex discrimination in educational programs and activities that receive federal funding, into law as part of the US Education Department's amendments. Great timing because I wanted to play Little League. My skills were honed each night with a game of catch with my dad. I was by far one of the best players as I could throw accurately, far, and I could hit. So I went to the school gym one night with my dad to sign up. We stood in line like every other boy and his father, and waited until we got to the front of the line at the long rectangular table.

The man behind the desk did not look up when he asked, "Name?" I confidently said, "Sherry Levin." That is when he looked up. He took off his reading glasses to get a better look at the kid standing in front of him. He paused and then said, "You cannot play. You are a girl." At that point, I turned to look at my dad, my superhero, to swoop in and be my savior. Tell them Dad. I can outrun, out hit, and outplay any of these boys. My dad pulled out a printed flier from his pocket, unfolded it to show the man. Nowhere on the flyer did it specify boys only. *Go Dad, you tell them,* I thought to myself. The man behind the desk then asked us to talk with him in the hall. Now in the hallway, away from the other fathers and their sons, the man said, "I am sorry, but Little League is for boys. We could put her in the Developmental Farm League but that is the best I can do." *NOT GOOD ENOUGH.* Farm league was for the kids who could not throw, run fast, or hit the ball. I was not going to do that.

I cried in the car on the way home. My dad assured me that it would be OK. His big hand hugged mine, "Someday you will have your chance." And he was right. Two years later, when I was in sixth grade, the GALS girls softball league formed. I joined as soon as I could. Two years was a long time to wait. But I batted clean-up, played first base, and my team won the league.

My competitive resolve and resilience reared up once again when I was in junior high school, which was grades seven through nine in our school system. The year was now 1975, and a girls' soccer team was formed. With high hopes I joined all the other players in practice. Without much training in organized youth soccer for girls, the skill level was not very high. I went home quite discouraged. Granted, it was only one practice, but I knew I had overall athletic skills and wanted to be challenged. My dad's response "Why don't you go and try out for the boys' team?" Seriously? Again? But this time it just so happened that the coach for the seventh-grade boys' team was my sister's English teacher. She said she would make the introduction.

The next day, we went to his classroom, and I presented my case. Then success. He was willing to give me a shot. That's all I needed to hear. If I could make it on the team, I could play. And make it I did! For my three years in junior high school, I played on the boys' soccer teams. I started each season, seventh, eighth, and varsity, and I led the team in scoring. Was I teased by the opponents? Yes, but my teammates were quick to rush to my defense. Did my teammates chuckle when we did chest trapping drills? Yes. It was certainly funny to fourteen-year-old boys.

In ninth grade, during my final game of playing boys' varsity soccer against the City All-Stars, one of the most horrifying moments of my life happened. We were leading the game 1-0 when the ball was kicked ahead toward the goal. I sprinted to it as it took a high bounce. Without hesitation, I jumped to head it toward the goal when CRACK. I was kicked in the face. A 6'2" lanky boy accidentally missed the ball and kicked me directly square in the face.

I lay on the ground as my right winger, Phou Chou, stood over me calling my name with his Filipino accent, "Sherry! Sherry!" The next thing I recall is my coach and my dad running toward me. My dad, in a heroic fashion, picked me up off the ground and helped me to the sideline. With blood streaming down my face,I was helped into my dad's car and driven to the hospital.

At the hospital emergency room, the doctors applied dilation drops to my eye. The blow broke my nose and fractured my eye socket. Once my dad heard "eye socket," he immediately asked for an eye specialist. Back in the car and a ride to a neighboring town.

I still can recall every detail of that night: Waiting outside the ophthalmologist's office with my dad's large overcoat draped over my slumping shoulders like a prize fighter's robe. I probably looked like a prize fighter, too, with all that blood all over my face and uniform. Still wearing my cleats, I leaned up against the front door of the medical building until they unlocked it. Fortunately for me, the ophthalmologist was working late and stayed open for me. He checked the integrity of my eye, which was excruciatingly painful, and then sent us home with many unanswered questions and a patch over my eye.

My mom understandably freaked out, and it turned into a full-blown scene. That night, my parents argued in the kitchen about whether I should have been allowed to play boys' soccer. My mom blamed my dad, but he stood his ground, insisting it was something I needed to do. And he was right. The competitive drive in me couldn't settle for anything less than playing at the highest level.

I wore that patch over my eye for weeks, waiting for the muscles around my eye socket to heal and the double vision to fade. It finally did, and thank goodness surgery was averted.

By tenth grade, my high school had a girls' soccer team. I became the leading scorer and was voted captain in my junior year. The resilience I'd developed from competing on the boys' team fueled my drive and would become the foundation for my future successes.

More battles to face. More wins to claim. More accolades to earn.

Each pre-game speech in this quarter concentrates on the concept of inner strength fueled by determination and the willful journey of controlling the controllables to take action.

King of the Mountain

When I was in elementary school, we used to play a game called, "King of the Mountain." In those winters that accumulated multiple inches of snow, the school parking lot snow banks would sometimes reach over ten feet tall. The rules of the game, or lack thereof, would be that one person would stand at the top and all the other participants would try to knock them off. The one who was successful would take reign as King of the Mountain.

We cannot rest. We cannot relax our efforts, no matter who we play. We have to expect that every team circles us on their schedule because beating us can make their season. My dad used to tell me that when you put your head above the crowd, people want to knock it off. So, be ready and give it your best every play, every game, every day. It would make the other team's season to beat us.

So, when you are on the top, when you are the King of the Mountain, you must do everything in your power to stay there!

As head coach at Worcester Academy, my teams secured four New England championships and finished as runners-up three times. At another private school, we achieved an undefeated season, captured the New England championship, and claimed the conference banner five times. Over my coaching career, I amassed 420 wins with just ninety-seven losses, achieving an impressive winning percentage of 81 percent.

With success, however, came a target on our backs. Every opponent brought their best effort, determined to take us down. As a result, sustaining that level of success required unwavering commitment. We had to show up every single day with focus, resilience, and the drive to be our absolute best—no excuses, no hesitation.

Life's journey is never a straight path. It's more like a rollercoaster with ups and downs, twists and turns. I always maintain that your life is not defined when things are going well; rather, it is defined by what you do when it is not!

To be honest, it is extremely difficult to show up at your best every day. I have days that I just want to close the computer and go on a hike away from all the pressures that go along with competing or performing. When that happens, I allow myself to have a moment to step away.

When I eventually identify what is causing me to feel this way, I am able to take a breath, focus on the issue, and come back stronger. So, call a friend, go on a walk, listen to music, and get back in the headspace to pick yourself up and start all over again.

All you can do is your best. And that's OK. Try not to measure yourself against what others accomplish. Instead, try to focus on what you can control.

One of my proudest moments that stemmed from my basketball career at Holy Cross was the incredible honor that was bestowed upon me as a result. It all began with an unexpected phone call from my Holy Cross classmate and friend, Ted Lynch. Ted and I had stayed in touch over the years, but this call in particular left me speechless and teary.

As our class co-chair, Ted had done some research and discovered that I still held the all-time scoring record for points at Holy Cross—2,253 points in just 103 games, all without the benefit of a three-point shot. This realization inspired him to take action. He reached out to other classmates, and together, they decided that my achievement deserved recognition at our upcoming thirty-fifth reunion. I was stunned. *WOW, this is amazing*, I thought.

Ted explained that he'd need to collaborate with the development and athletic departments to determine what the honor would look like. That call came in the winter of 2019, and I was thrilled at the thought of my beloved coach, Togo Palazzi, being present for the celebration.

However, life threw us some curveballs. The athletic department underwent leadership changes, delaying the plans. Then came the COVID-19 pandemic, an unforeseen challenge that postponed everything further. Through it all, Ted remained steadfast, determined to see this through.

Finally, after two years of back-and-forth planning, Ted called me again with incredible news:

"We have a date—November 19, 2021."

"Yay!" I replied, my excitement building.

"And we know what we'd like to do. We'd like to name the lounge in the locker room after you."

"Wow," I said, overwhelmed with gratitude.

Ted continued, "In typical Holy Cross tradition, we'd have a priest bless the space."

"Fabulous!" I replied. "I'd love Father Markey to do this, if possible."

Father Markey, a longtime friend, supporter, and someone I hold dear, had been the Dean of Students during my time at Holy Cross. While I was an Academic All-American, I had a few nervous moments in his office. Father Markey had also been a teammate of Togo's, captain of the Class of 1953 team, and remained an ardent supporter of our women's basketball program. Over the years, we'd stayed connected at various events, and I was even honored to attend his ninetieth birthday celebration.

Then Ted asked, "Would you like to have a Rabbi there as well?"

My heart swelled with emotion, and tears filled my eyes. This gesture was a profound acknowledgment of who I am. I had attended Holy Cross with a strong Jewish faith, seamlessly fitting into their Jesuit world. Their respect for my beliefs, paired with my admiration for their teachings, created a beautiful bond of mutual understanding.

"Yes," I replied, my voice shaking. "I do have a close family Rabbi." Just as I gathered myself, Ted asked one final question: "Would you like to have a mezuzah hung on the doorpost of the locker room?"

That was it. The floodgates opened. I couldn't have imagined a more meaningful gesture. With tears streaming down my face, I replied, "Yes, that would be so special."

Finally, the day arrived. Surrounded by friends, classmates, teammates, family, Togo, Father Markey, and our Rabbi, the Sherry Levin Women's Basketball Lounge was officially named in my honor. Father Markey spoke with heartfelt eloquence, his words resonating deeply, not only to me as a player but unbeknownst to him, were the essence of *Pre-Game*:

"We bless this locker room and honor Sherry Levin in doing
so. A locker room is a special place, almost a sanctuary, and
not merely a place where one prepares for the contest; it is a
place reserved only for coach and players. It is a place where
a coach can teach, instruct, correct errors, and motivate each
member of a team to offer their talent and energy for the
goal of victory. But it is also a place where players are free to
talk, socialize, and change the course of teammates.

It is a place where players share humor, encouragement, amid
tensions, and mental preparation. It is a place not open to
outsiders and spectators, not even the press unless invited in.
It is a private place for the coach and the team, and what
is said here, spoken behind closed doors, must stay here. It is
a place where players and coaches can bond as one. Where
each mind and heart is one. It is here that their mission at
hand becomes clear as the motivation intended. It is more
than a locker room; it is a special place, almost a sanctuary.

So, today we honor Sherry because she as much as any player
made this sacred space to all that was mentioned."

Following Father Markey's blessings was the ceremonial hanging of the mezuzah. This particular mezuzah held a unique significance—it had been donated by another Jewish student who had cherished it, saying, "I was saving this for a special moment, and this is the one."

We all gathered outside the locker room door, an air of reverence and excitement surrounding us. With my arms raised and a screwdriver in hand, I carefully tightened the screws into the pre-drilled holes while the Rabbi recited the blessing in Hebrew, his voice resonating with tradition and spirituality.

I know that the vast majority of players, coaches, and recruits who enter the locker room may notice the mezuzah but not fully grasp its sacred meaning. Yet for the few who pause to take a closer look, they will find a plaque beside it that reads:

*"The mezuzah, which was placed here in honor of Sherry
Levin '84, contains biblical essentials of faith and is a
Jewish doorpost symbol of God's presence in our midst. It is
a reminder that as we pass through this threshold to find
spiritual shelter as we enter, and to take with us as we exit,
the divine values and guidance to make the world a better
place."*

In that moment, I felt blessed, grateful, and truly felt like I was the
King of the Mountain.

Patience, Patience, Patience

When I was young, yes, kind of one of those stories that your grandparents tell about walking to school two miles both ways uphill—when I had a research paper to write I had to go to the library. It took all day to complete the process of looking through a card catalog of the books in the library that might, just might be applicable to my report, write that book title and catalog number on a form, and hand it to the librarian. Then wait...wait...wait, finally getting the stack of books you asked for, bringing them back to your desk, taking some bits of pertinent information, and then realizing you need more. The process would start all over again. Sounds exhausting? It was. At the end of a day when you would call your parents from the pay phone to pick you up, your research was complete.

This makes me sound ancient, I know. But that slow process taught my generation patience and discipline.

Basketball works the same way. The game isn't won in the first minute, or the tenth, or twentieth. You win at minute thirty-two, at the buzzer. You need patience—on offense to read what the defense gives you, on defense to learn each player's tendencies. Make the right adjustments and you'll find success. One play, one possession, one second—it all matters. Be patient through the game's natural rhythm.

Patience, patience, patience.

It's only natural that with all the information at our fingertips that we could ever want or need, people can be impatient. When we don't get what we want within the snap of a finger, we get stressed and frustrated to the point where we just simply give up.

Remember, everything worthwhile that you do in life takes time. The time to process, assess, and implement. Reacting hastily to a situation can lead to disastrous results. The old act of counting to ten before you speak takes patience. Another one of those easier said than done practices.

So, too, does accomplishing most things in life. Building a positive relationship takes patience. Sometimes people have to grow together and learn about each other's strengths and weaknesses before accepting the person for who they are. This takes patience. I would tell my daughter, "If you are waiting for a perfect friend, you won't have any." No one is perfect. Acceptance takes time. Understanding takes patience.

I had a tradition of giving my senior players the Dr. Seuss book, *Oh, The Places You'll Go!*, when they graduated. I love the simplicity of the words in this book, matched with the profound message. One passage that always resonated with me speaks to embracing both success and setback—the reality that we'll soar to incredible heights, yet sometimes we'll stumble. Both are part of the journey. In the book, Dr. Seuss wrote:

> *"Wherever you fly, you'll be the best of the best.*
> *Wherever you go, you will top all the rest.*
> *Except when you don't.*
> *Because, sometimes, you won't."*

My heart warmed when I saw that one of my former players, Gisemi, had placed the book I gave her on the bookshelf in her twin babies' room. She cherished that book just as much as I treasured the journey we shared. It was a beautiful reminder of the positive impact we can have on one another's lives. Gisemi remains a special person in my life. Years later, another player, Oluchi, told me she brings the book with her wherever her journey takes her. A reminder of the highs and inevitable stumbles.

Life is a constant ebb and flow. Embrace both, knowing they are part of the journey. Move swiftly through the lows with resilience, and savor the highs with gratitude, for they are what make the ride so meaningful.

The not-yet mentality reframes skill development as a journey rather than a limitation or destination. Instead of saying, "I can't shoot a pull-up jumpshot," say, "I'm not yet proficient at it." Rather than "I'm a bad cook," say,

"I'm not yet a good chef." Or instead of, "I can't figure out this problem," say, "I'm not yet there, and I will try again." This simple shift in perspective fosters a sense of progress, resilience, and optimism, reminding us that growth is always possible with effort and persistence. All of them take time.

In 2023, I had the distinct privilege of being a keynote speaker at the Female Athlete Conference in Boston, Massachusetts. I admit that until I did research on the event, I did not know it was founded in 2013 by Kate Ackerman, MD, MPH, FACSM. Dr. Kate is another strong, intelligent, powerful woman. Their website boasts that the conference "continues to be the preeminent summit, building strong networks while highlighting evidence to empower female athletes across the lifespan. It also provides the opportunity for those committed to the health and performance of female athletes to gather, exchange ideas, and advance our knowledge within the field."

During my calls with the organizers, I immediately felt at ease. Laura Reece and Grace Saville guided me every step of the way. My daughter helped me organize my story so that it would be impactful to the wide variety of audiences of "top researchers, healthcare providers, thought-leaders, athletes, coaches, and advocates from around the globe attend to advance female health and performance at all levels." As someone who does my research and preparation, I attended the conference the day before I was to speak so I would get the understanding of this amazing event. And, whoah! I was blown away.

After hearing the depth of research and the inspirational speeches, I knew I had to be on top of my game too! It turned out to be one of my favorite speeches; I stood in front of 1,300 people for forty-five minutes. Some of my friends would joke, "Forty-five minutes? Is that enough for you?" I built my narrative with these five pillars and called them my:

Aha Moments

- ✓ Keep Your Eyes, Mind, and Heart Wide Open
- ✓ Authenticity is Your Superpower
- ✓ Pivot or Push
- ✓ We are Stronger Together
- ✓ Go All In

Each one of these aha moments has shown up in a pre-game speech in one way or another. The common thread connecting them all is time—each insight required patience to grow and be nurtured before it could take root.

After my keynote speech, I sat in the hotel lobby feeling both proud and emotionally spent. A woman approached to congratulate me and share how much my presentation had inspired her. She sat down, and we fell into conversation about the conference. I learned she held a doctorate from Edinburgh, Scotland. As we talked, I confessed my awe at being surrounded by so many brilliant people with impressive credentials and strings of initials after their names. My new friend leaned in with her thick Scottish accent and said, "But you should add QBE to your name."

Surprised, I asked, "Really? Is that a thing? That's cool. What's QBE?"

"Qualified by Experience," she replied.

Those three words stopped me in my tracks. I loved it. And honestly, it was quite true. When I look at my journey—the resilience I've built, the successes I've earned, the heartbreak I've endured, and the joy I've discovered—all of these stories have given me a wealth of experience. And over time, with patience, that experience has crystallized into insights to share which takes me back to my first aha moment- Keep Your Eyes, Mind, and Heart Wide Open!

Patience, patience, patience. That's what turns experience into wisdom.

Build the Foundation

There are so many sayings to buttress this idea, but the one that first came to my mind is, "You have to crawl before you can walk." So simple, yet think of how many times this quote is a reality. There has to be a starting point to build on in everything we do. Learning to write, one needs to learn the alphabet. Learning geometry, one needs to learn addition. Even in a relationship, you have to build a strong foundation of trust before you can truly be authentic. The idea of not yet allows for growth and development.

In developmental psychology, there is research that states, "A baby's brain begins developing before birth and, in the early years, significant 'wiring' occurs within the brain, effectively programming the child's development. Between two to six months, a baby will learn about emotions through watching how you react to them when they coo, cry, smile, or yell." and "From birth to age five, a child's brain is growing at warp speed. Neurological and brain development in early childhood is shaped by every interaction children have. Even experiences that may seem insignificant to an adult, like meeting a new person, teach a child how to interact with the world around them. That's because the brain's size and shape are constantly changing in response to encounters during this period." I find this quite intimidating. What a huge responsibility it is to get it right! To make sure the foundation is strong enough to allow positive growth in the next stages of development. Wow!

Of course, on a positive note, with a strong foundation built, I believe that anything can be tackled. Think about your career, your job. Now, think about your next job. If you have established a firm base of competency and knowledge, you can progress easily to the next phase. Even if it is in a different genre, you can continue to be supported by your experiences of yesterday.

People talk about impostor syndrome, which is the condition of feeling anxious and not experiencing success internally, despite being high-performing in external, objective ways. This condition often results in people feeling like a fraud and doubting their abilities. Women, unfortunately, tend to feel this more than men.

Have you felt this way? I have. Self-doubt and insecurities creep in at times. Then I remember all the hard work and the effort that I have put into something. Remind yourself of the fortress you built. If, for some reason, you don't get the job or the win, as long as you give it your best, you can walk away with your head held high. No regrets.

Once I chose basketball as my sport to dedicate my life's mission, I set my sights on being a member of the USA Olympic team. My Why drove my actions of being in the best shape I could be, getting proper sleep and nutrition, and sometimes making the tough decision to not participate in college social events in order to be rested before a game. These were hard choices, but I knew that in the end, it was following my dream.

One key principle I've embraced in my coaching—and in life—is setting clear expectations before making judgments. In basketball, for instance, there are multiple ways to defend a ball handler, but I teach my players to direct them toward the sideline or baseline. By first establishing this foundational technique, I can fairly hold them accountable when they don't execute it correctly. This approach extends far beyond sports. Whether in leadership, parenting, education, or personal growth, providing clear guidance upfront allows for constructive correction rather than unfair criticism. When people understand what's expected, they have a framework for success—and when they fall short, they have a clear path for improvement.

The world is moving at a pace that's impossible to keep up with. AI has changed the way we learn, write, and create. The way I learned in school is totally different from today's classrooms, and we can't even fathom what's next. Think about the warp speed of knowledge being launched—ChatGPT was introduced to the public on November 30, 2022, and we're already living in a different world. Without a crystal ball to predict what's coming, the important thing is to build a foundation of curiosity and love of learning. If you can continue to explore new aspects of learning, you'll be able to enjoy education no matter how much it changes.

Building a strong foundation is essential for lasting success in any endeavor. Whether in sports, education, relationships, or personal growth, solid groundwork provides the stability and clarity needed to navigate challenges and build upon progress. Without it, efforts become unfocused and unsustainable. A well-established foundation not only sets clear expectations but also fosters confidence, resilience, and continuous improvement.

Togo used to say, "what you did last week, last month, and last year will help you next week, next month, and next year." I would always take this to heart both as a player and a coach. I knew that team activities in the summer would contribute to our success during the season. We would establish a strong foundation for coming together when it mattered the most.

So next time you head out to build a proverbial snowman, remember this little tip—start with a strong base, just like in life! A sturdy foundation keeps your frosty friend standing tall, no matter how windy it gets.

Play Every Play

In 2004, we were playing in the NEPSAC Championship—a defining moment for our program. In my first two seasons, we fought our way to the championship game, but it was in my third season that we finally achieved victory.

That game was intense, with every play magnified in importance. My best post player was battling for an offensive rebound in a critical moment. She couldn't secure the ball or even get a solid hand on it. All she managed was a single fingertip grazing the ball, just enough to alter its trajectory. That slight touch redirected the ball into the hands of her teammate, who immediately went up for the shot, scored, and was fouled.

That three-point play proved to be the turning point, sealing Worcester Academy's first-ever girls basketball NEPSAC Championship. It was a testament to perseverance and effort. Had my post player given up on the rebound or decided her effort didn't matter, we might have lost. Instead, her fingertip—her refusal to quit—made all the difference.

Play every play like it's the most important play of the game. You never know which one it might be!

This is a powerful example of how the smallest actions can create the biggest impact. Think about it, there's an irony in life: You never know which moment, decision, or experience will end up being the difference maker. So, why not give your all in every one of them?

Life often surprises us with the unexpected. It's in those seemingly insignificant moments—the ones we might overlook—that the seeds of greatness are planted. A simple smile to a stranger might brighten their day in ways you'll never know. A brief word of encouragement to a friend could inspire them to chase their dreams. And holding the door for someone or lending a listening ear might feel small to you, but to the recipient, it could be monumental.

This principle applies to the joyful moments as well as the big challenges. Unexpected acts of kindness can bring a profound sense of personal satisfaction. It's the handwritten thank-you note that strengthens a relationship, the spontaneous gesture that creates a lifelong memory, or the extra hour spent helping a colleague that earns their trust and respect.

In sports, it's about the hustle plays like diving for a loose ball that can change the entire outcome of the game. In business, it's taking the time to triple-check a report's spelling that can prevent a costly mistake. In a relationship, it's making a small gesture to let the other person know just how much you care that can strengthen your bond.

Of course, the big moments matter too. But the beauty of life is that the little ones—the ones we don't anticipate—can sometimes bring the most joy or leave the most lasting impression. That's why it's essential to approach each moment with care, intention, and mindfulness.

My high school, Newton North, spanned grades ten through twelve, and I was a varsity athlete in soccer, basketball, and track and field each season I competed. During my sophomore year, our basketball team was made up of mostly upperclassmen. Although they were older, only one player was planning to play in college. The team had finished around .500 the previous year, but with my added skills and a few other young talents, we were hopeful to qualify for the state tournament.

Despite having confidence in my abilities, I was nervous during tryouts, as the upperclassmen were a tight-knit group and protective of one another. Only one player, Laura—our best post player—took me under her wing. Sensing my nerves as we stood against the wall waiting for our turn on the court, she tried to ease my tension with a joke.

"What did Tarzan say when he saw the elephants running over the hill?" she asked.

I shook my head, unsure how to respond.

She grinned and said, "He said, 'Look, the elephants are coming over the hill!'"

I gave a small laugh, and then she added, "What did Tarzan say when the elephants were coming over the hill but wearing sunglasses?"

Now smiling, I played along, "What?"

She delivered the punchline: "He didn't say anything because he didn't recognize them!"

That silly joke was exactly what I needed to lighten the moment. I went on to make the varsity team and eventually earned All-Star recognition.

We won our first game of the season, and I was the leading scorer with fifteen points. However, our second game was a different story. We traveled to face Cambridge Rindge and Latin, one of the top teams in the state. The gym, located in the heart of Cambridge, Massachusetts, was packed with students who screamed nonstop throughout the game. We were outmatched from the start. Medina Dixon, a 6'2" powerhouse who later became my teammate on the Amateur Athletic Union (AAU) Boston Blazers (the one and only AAU team in New England), an eventual national champion at Old Dominion, and an Olympian, dominated the court with her presence and shot-blocking ability. Intimidated, I altered my shot, changing its arc to avoid her blocks. I scored only two points, and we lost.

The loss was hard, but my poor performance devastated me. I knew I was better than that. Determined to improve, I went to the high school's open gym the next day. First, I focused on regaining my shooting touch. Then I practiced off-the-dribble moves to create more space for my shots. Finally, I joined the pickup games, the only girl playing among men. I tolerated the sweaty bellies of the "skins" team because I knew every play, every game, was making me stronger.

My hard work paid off. Later in the season, we defeated Cambridge Rindge and Latin on our home court and qualified for the state tournament. We advanced to the second round before losing to Wellesley High School. Unfortunately, Laura wasn't able to play. In a twist of bad luck, she slipped a disk playing charades in the locker room before the first round. Yes, you read that correctly—charades! Our coach, trying to pass the time before the game, had suggested it. Although we managed to win that first game without her, her absence in the second round was a blow we couldn't overcome. To this day, I can't stand playing charades!

That season taught me a powerful lesson. One game, one mistake, or even one bad moment doesn't define you. It's what you choose to do afterward that matters. I used that challenging game against Cambridge Rindge and Latin as fuel to improve. I learned to flip an "L" from representing a "loss" to standing for a "lesson."

In life, the smallest ripple—a joke that lightens a moment, a decision to work harder, or a lesson learned from failure—can grow into the biggest wave. So, make them all count. You never know which will have lasting implications.

Good Isn't Good When Better Is Expected

Surprisingly, desk blotters still exist. For those unfamiliar, these large cardboard, paper, or leather mats once protected desks from typewriter scratches—think of typewriters as laptops with paper and ink rollers.

On my college desk blotter, I had written: "Good isn't good when better is expected."

The expectation to be better is something I always strive to accomplish. So should we. We are talented and driven. We need to push through doubts and mistakes not to settle.

I'm not asking you to do anything beyond your capabilities. Play within yourself. Go to your strengths. Do that, and together we'll reach our potential. Be the best version of yourself.

In life, we naturally gravitate toward activities and pursuits where we experience success. I have admired former Oklahoma Women's Basketball Coach Sherri Coale as a coach and now follow her blogs. She captured this perfectly in her blog: "I used to tell my players to follow what they were good at until it ran into what they loved. The intersection would be their sweet spot, the place where they would thrive." Beautifully written.

I can still recall how much I hated the gymnastics program in elementary school. For me, it was like nails on a chalkboard. Why? Because I wasn't flexible, and I was terrified of doing a flip. When the gym teacher announced we all had to participate, I braced for humiliation. But then I discovered something—I could vault with the best of them. I could sprint like lightning to the springboard, launch into the air, and soar over the horse, landing solidly on the thin mat.

This moment taught me that loving what you do often stems from doing what you're good at. It's about finding that activity that makes you leap out of bed with excitement, as if every day were a GAME DAY.

The concept of being good when better is expected resonates deeply with me. When you excel at something, there's an implicit challenge to maintain that level of excellence. If you're an "A" student, a "B" feels like failure. In sports, I've seen this firsthand. When one of my players wins a sprint at practice, I always ask, "Do you know what that means?" They usually don't and look at me with inquisitive stares. So I tell them, "It means you're capable of winning every sprint. And if you don't, ask yourself—did you really try your best?"

During our 2017–18 championship season, this mindset was ingrained in my team. My players weren't just talented—they were fiercely competitive. They wanted to win, even in practice. That relentless drive created an environment where each player pushed themselves and each other to be their absolute best.

At the heart of this drive was Aliyah Boston, a 6'4" junior at the time. Aliyah wasn't just a dominant presence on the court; she was meticulous in every sense. She demanded excellence from herself in every drill, every play, and yes, even in every sprint.

But Aliyah wasn't the only one raising the bar. Our guards—quick, determined, and hungry to prove themselves—loved giving her a run for her money. Adara, one of our fiercest competitors, always brought her A-game. I nicknamed her "My Travel Buddy" because of the time we spent together representing Team USA at the Pan Am Maccabi Games in Budapest and the World Maccabiah Games in Israel. Tough as nails, Adara later played Division I basketball at New Hampshire and South Dakota.

Then there was Leilani, a firecracker of a guard whose grit and determination were unmatched. On defense, Leilani was a force of nature. She could lock down an opponent like no one I've ever coached, forcing turnovers and disrupting plays with her relentless energy.

Watching Aliyah, Adara, and Leilani race each other during practice-ending sprints was a spectacle. They pushed each other to the limit, refusing to give an inch. I'd stand at the baseline, eyes locked on the finish line, just to see who'd come out on top.

This spirit of competition wasn't just about winning games—it was about building a culture of excellence and mutual respect. Our success came not only from talent but from the relentless pursuit of improvement and the bonds we formed along the way. We tackled every day with high expectations.

Off the court, I prioritized fostering a strong team connection. Pre-practice locker room meetings were a cornerstone of this effort. I'd start with a simple prompt, and each player would share their thoughts. I participated too, always honest and authentic, modeling the vulnerability I hoped to inspire in them.

One evening, during one of these moments of connection, Adara noticed a small black speck just below my neck. She pointed it out, and for a brief moment, I was caught off guard, embarrassed, thinking I was going to brush off a crumb from dinner. Then I remembered—it was one of three small tattoos, not a fashion statement or a rebellious moment; the tiny marks were tattoos from the radiation therapy I underwent during my battle with breast cancer.

In that unplanned moment, I shared a part of my story. Those marks weren't just remnants of a challenging chapter; they were symbols of resilience, strength, and the determination to keep moving forward. Just as I expected my players to push themselves to be their best, I had pushed myself to overcome life's hurdles.

One of my favorite players—and people—is Oluchi. She transferred to Worcester Academy as a junior from another prep school, and her godfather, Chris, another of the quality persons in this world, who knew my reputation for coaching high-level athletes, helped make it all happen. From the moment she arrived, the work began. Oluchi was coachable, driven, and eager to improve. She didn't just want to be good; she wanted to be great. Together, we transformed her game, shifting her from a 5'10" small forward into a dynamic guard who could control the game and score. It was a process that required patience, discipline, and relentless effort—something she continues to refine every day.

During one of our team bonding exercises, "Baggage Claim," where players share something they want to let go of to lighten their mental load, the responses ranged from typical school stress to minor family conflicts to the disappointing lunch meal. When it was Oluchi's turn, she quietly admitted, "I don't want to disappoint Coach." A collective "Aww" filled the room, but I knew this moment required a deeper conversation.

After practice, I pulled her aside and reassured her, "Oluchi, you will <u>never</u> disappoint me as long as you give your best effort." We hugged, and in that moment, I knew just how much our connection meant to her and to me. Her natural talent set the bar high, and her expectations would fuel her pursuit, but it was her commitment to growth that made her truly special. I embraced the responsibility of guiding her, pushing her, and helping her reach her full potential.

Her dedication paid off. Oluchi earned a scholarship to Duke University, and after just one season, she was honored as the Atlantic Coast Conference (ACC) Sixth Player of the Year. It was an incredible achievement, not just for a freshman, but for any player in the conference. In her sophomore year, she was named the ACC Tournament MVP and has now transferred to Maryland to continue to pursue her dream of winning a national championship.

Oluchi's journey is a testament to the power of hard work, belief, and the willingness to embrace the process of greatness. Oluchi did not accept the idea of being good enough; she wanted to embrace the expectations of greatness. I am blessed to have been able to coach a person like Oluchi, and I know she will always be a part of my life. In her own words, she gave me the greatest honor as a coach:

> *"...the confidence and joy you instilled in me makes me so grateful. I know whenever things are challenging in my career, you'll be right there ready to lift me up. I am so blessed I get to have you in my corner, and whenever things are tough, I always remember to SMILE! Love you endlessly, Coach."*

Ultimately, it's not just about winning games or hitting milestones. It's about giving your all in everything you do, embracing challenges, and letting even the smallest victories remind you of your strength. Because when you strive to be your best, you inspire others to do the same.

Create Your Own Narrative

> *It's amazing how many decisions we make in a day without even realizing it. Stop and notice. What time you wake up is your first decision that you make the night before. Once you open your eyes, do you reach for your phone? What are your first thoughts? Your morning routine of brushing teeth, putting on makeup, etc., is all planned. What you eat for breakfast and how you speak to the person in your house. The route you drive to school to work. And so on and so on...you are in control.*
>
> *On the court, you make a decision every second of every play. How you defend, who you pass to, the move you make with the ball, etc. These decisions are made consciously and without thinking. The practice you put in day after day gives you the ability not to have to think. That's the part you design. Those are the best ones because you put the time into making them muscle memory. That's when you will be at your best!!*

Ask yourself, when you are meeting someone for the first time at a party or event, what information do you share? Really getting to know someone takes time. Think about those awkward first dates. You know the basic elevator speech questions: Where did you grow up? What school did you attend? Where have you traveled lately? What teams do you root for? I could go on and on, but I am sure you get my drift. What is fascinating is that the answers to these questions shape the person you are at that moment. Then, as you dig deeper, think of the times you told someone a childhood memory. Ever think, "Why did that memory stick with me?" For example, why did I retain the story of me eating pancakes every gameday in college? Why did having lunch with my grandmother and sister every Saturday stay with me? As we grow older, we lose some of our memories, but the ones we hold dear are the ones that make us who we are.

Dr. Chantel Prat, a neuroscientist from the University of Washington, was the mainstage speaker at the 2022 Generation W signature event. During her presentation, she said, "You are neither an actor in, nor the passive observer of your reality. <u>You are the creator of it.</u>" This understanding gives one the power over your choices and control over your actions..

My daughter and I often marvel at the life we've built together, sharing special moments as a single mom and her growing child. From an early age, she had no choice but to tag along with me to basketball practices, games, trips, and camps. Those experiences gave her a front-row seat to see her mom—and other women coaches—taking charge, leading with determination, and navigating the highs and lows of life. Marcia witnessed me being upset, joyful, and inspirational, learning more from those moments than I could have imagined.

One funny memory stands out as proof that she was always listening, even if she didn't quite grasp the nuances of what she heard. When Marcia was about four years old, she was playing with her blocks, something she loved to do. Suddenly, she stopped and asked for my help: "Mom, can you help me put this round peg into the square hole? I can't do it." Naturally, I couldn't either. I explained gently, "No, it won't fit. It's the wrong shape." Her response left me speechless yet with a sneaky chuckle: "But Mom, you can do anything you set your mind to. Don't give up—you can do it." I froze, realizing she had absorbed my locker room pep talks to my team. Though she didn't fully understand their context, she had internalized the message that persistence matters.

It's memories like these that I cherish and reflect on often. My friends and family laugh at how I often start a conversation with, "Oh, remember when...?" Most times, they don't recall the details, so I've become their unofficial memory bank. I also recommend keeping a journal to document the everyday moments, big and small—your travels, milestones, even the drive toward a career path. These are treasures, just for you, until one day you choose to share them.

The locker room was always a sacred space for my teams—a place where players could be their authentic selves. Each year, the unique mix of personalities created a team dynamic unlike any other. Off the court, they bonded in ways only they could. But on the court, I liked to think the team reflected their coach's personality. I hoped that meant they played with intensity and passion.

Before every game, I'd deliver these pre-game speeches, outlining our keys to victory. The final bullet points were always the same:

PLAY HARD. BE SMART. <u>RUN, RUN, RUN.</u> AND HAVE FUN!!!

Some of my players were incredibly superstitious. They'd insist on the exact number of underlined words or exclamation points I'd used in previous games. Sometimes, I'd forget something on purpose, just to let them correct me and get a laugh.

The 2006 team was one of the closest-knit groups I've ever coached. The captains, Laticia and Gisemi Rolle, were half sisters and extraordinary leaders. On the court, they were an extension of my voice, while off the court, they created a culture of love and camaraderie. We were truly a family who loved each other.

At the time, my life as a single mom was a whirlwind of stress and juggling. Marcia would often travel 150 miles to visit her father in Connecticut on alternating weekends. I had to hire drivers to take her there and back when I had games. During the season, she'd attend practices with her sitter or accompany me to games. The team embraced her as their little sister, and she adored them, looking up to them as mentors and role models. We cannot control how other people behave, but we can control our reactions and response. Supporting the idea that we create our own narrative.

On Valentine's Day, Marcia and I put together a Happiness Kit for each player. Something I would repeat most years with all the teams until my marble supply ran out. The Happiness Kits were little bags that included:

✓ A marble: for when you feel like you've lost all yours.
✓ A rubber band: to stretch your limits.
✓ An eraser: to make your troubles disappear.

✓ A piece of string: to remind us we're tied together.

✓ A chocolate kiss: so you remember someone loves you.

✓ A penny: so you'll never be broke.

The 2006 team responded with their own, though not quite as sentimental, gift for me: a Grow a Boyfriend novelty toy. The package read: "Mr. Right can grow up to 600% of his size in water. He never snores, never looks at your credit card bill, and always agrees with you." We laughed and laughed. He "lived" in the Gatorade cooler we borrowed from the training room, growing larger every day, until we had to return the cooler for actual use.

Another fun item to keep us pepped during the season , and was quite funny, was the Staples "That Was Easy" button. We hung it in the locker room and pressed it after every win. It received many presses, as we finished undefeated at 24–0.

To foster teamwork and celebrate effort, I introduced the Charge Card. It was a laminated card I'd give to players who charged in a game. Rashonda "Ro" Speed practically collected all of them, averaging at least one charge per game.

I knew that this team was special. I intentionally left no stone unturned. We attended women's college basketball games, WNBA games, visited the Basketball Hall of Fame in Springfield, Massachusetts, went to New England Revolution soccer games, watched movies, and ate dinners together. Our narrative at the end of the season was to put our heart and soul into being the best we could be. "I believe I can, I believe I will," was our mantra.

We are who we are by the choices we make each day—hundreds of them from the moment we wake to the moment we lie down. We create our own narrative. We control our own destiny. We can make the best out of situations if you shift your lens to be a positive one. My experiences helped to shape the lens that I look through, as did the voice of my esteemed head coach at Holy Cross, Togo Palazzi. My parents' love and support allowed me to be me and focus on my pursuits. Even playing clarinet in the wind ensemble, the marching band, and the show orchestra guided me to be disciplined with an appreciation for excellence.

The best advice: control what you can control. No one else is writing your story.

Following my breast cancer treatment in 2015, I was fortunate to connect with two incredible organizations that helped me reclaim my physical strength and mental fortitude: WeCanRow Boston and Haymakers for Hope. Both empowered me to take control and rewrite my reality on my own terms.

Keep your eyes, mind, and heart wide open and be receptive to allowing yourself to be fully in the present. You never know what moment will make a lasting memory!

THIRD QUARTER

Resilience

The gymnasium lights hummed overhead as sneakers squeaked against the hardwood. It was the night before the tournament—our final Friday night practice before heading to the Northfield Mount Hermon Holiday Tournament. The energy in the gym was high as we readied ourselves for what would prove to be a competitive weekend. Fun too, as we would stay overnight and enjoy team building. Talented teams from across the Northeast would be there, programs we'd only seen on highlight reels, and we were anxious to see how we measured up against the best—not just in New England, but beyond.

"Feed the post!" I called out, clapping my hands together. One of my favorite drills, and the girls knew it. The setup was simple but demanding: Guards dribbled down the sideline with on ball defensive pressure bearing down on them while the post players sprinted to the block. That's where I waited, football blocking pad in hand, ready to push them and make them work for position. The drill calls for the post to plant their foot and execute a reverse pivot into me so they can seal me—the defense—on their back. Get low, use your body, establish position. The more physical, the better. Sometimes, my post players are so strong, I get knocked back a few steps, so I always brace myself for contact.

It's always a fun drill with endless options to execute and improve. Everything was clicking that night, our team filled with the kind of sharp energy that comes right before a big weekend. Passes were crisp. Footwork was clean. Communication was loud. Then here comes my post player, full speed down the lane. I dig in, pad ready for impact. She plants her foot to make her move, but this time—this time—she plants it right on the inside of my ankle.

The pain shot up my leg like lightning. "Ouch!"

I sucked in air through my teeth. "Okay, okay," I managed, waving off the drill. "Let's reset." But I knew immediately something was wrong. My ankle screamed with each step as I limped to the sideline. One of our managers handed me a bag of ice without me having to ask—bless her—and I wrapped it around my ankle, already feeling the swelling begin. But we still had forty-five minutes of practice left, and we were leaving in the morning. So I stayed on my feet, coached through the pain, and moved gingerly along the court.

"Worcester!" we yelled in our closing huddle, left hands stacked in the center. Always left hand in, by the way—closer to the heart. The team then broke with a unified shout and ran off to the locker room, their voices echoing off the walls.

I finally allowed myself to sit. The ice had shifted, so I unwrapped it and started to readjust. That's when my assistant coach walked over, took one look, and gasped. "Yikes! Look at the size of your ankle."

I looked down. She was right. My ankle had ballooned to nearly twice its normal size, the skin already turning an impressive shade of purple. The ice had been no match for gravity and the swelling that comes from standing on an injury for forty-five minutes.

I hobbled to the training room, each step a negotiation with my body. Our trainer took one look and shook her head. "You need an X-ray. Tonight."

And of course, it was my right ankle. My driving foot. No way I'd be driving my car, never mind the team van, for a two-hour trip to the tournament.

Adjust. Be resilient. Laugh.

Those three words became my mantra as I sat there in the training room, never mind figuring out the logistics of how on earth we were going to get everything done. My assistant coach—a saint—graciously offered to drive me home and take me to the hospital. I sent a late-night email to the athletic director asking if a faculty member would be willing to travel with us over the weekend to help with driving.

After a few hours in the ER waiting room, I was relieved to hear there was no fracture. "Just a bad sprain," the doctor said, though the word "just" seemed to underestimate the angry, swollen mess that was my ankle. "Stay off it as much as possible." I left with my ankle professionally wrapped, a pair of metal crutches, and instructions I knew I couldn't fully follow. I had a team to coach.

The next morning, we loaded up and ventured to NMH for the tournament. I sat in the passenger seat with my leg elevated on a duffel bag, crutches wedged awkwardly behind my seat. More adjustments, resiliency, and laughter would be called upon. But I had no idea how much.

We drew one of the top girls' basketball programs in the country in our first game: Blair Academy. A powerhouse. NMH had two different gyms to accommodate the multi-day schedule, and our game was assigned to the smaller auxiliary court. But here was the kicker: no thirty-second shot clock. A throwback to the early days of competitive girls' high school basketball, when there was no clock to dictate pace on offense nor how long you had to shoot. Time itself became a weapon you could wield.

As I watched the Blair Academy girls warm up, going through their layup lines with precision and speed, it was obvious to both my assistant coach and me that we were overmatched. They looked more athletic, more skilled, and more polished than we were. Every movement was crisp, every shot smooth. These girls had probably been in elite programs since middle school.

I stood at half court, crutches tucked under each armpit, my throbbing ankle a constant reminder of the previous night, and I started scheming. How could we possibly compete?

Less speed. Less skill. No shot clock. Small court. Hmmmmm...

The equation formed in my mind. Only one strategy to employ: We had to take the air out of the ball. In non-basketball terms, slow the game down to a crawl. Frustrate them. Make them impatient. Give them fewer possessions, fewer opportunities to showcase their superior talent.

I called my team over, and they huddled around me, eyes wide. This wasn't what we'd practiced. This wasn't our normal game. "Listen," I said, leaning on my crutches, "we're going to do something different today. We're going to control the tempo. No shot clock means we decide when to shoot. We're going to be patient, move the ball, and only take the best shots. Make them chase us."

I called in my point guard and said, "I know we can do this. You got this."

She nodded and said, "Yes, Coach. Let's go!"

The first half went exactly as planned. We walked the ball up the court deliberately. Passed it around the perimeter. Reset the offense. Passed some more. The Blair girls swiped at the ball, reached, and the whistles came—foul after foul. Their frustration mounted with each passing minute. I could see it in their body language, hear it in their voices. Meanwhile, we played our game, methodical and controlled.

At halftime, the score read 14–12. The lowest-scoring half of my entire coaching career. We were ahead by a bucket. I looked at my girls in the locker room, and they were smiling, energized. They'd bought in completely.

I'd hoped to gain a bit of extra sympathy from the officials after they saw me hobbling around on crutches, but instead I'd discovered a new way to show my displeasure with calls. Instead of my usual heel stomp—impossible now—I had two aluminum crutches to bang on the floor. The hollow metallic clang echoed through the small gym. Quite satisfying to me, though, judging by the looks I was getting from the officiating crew, most likely annoying to them.

Our Freeze the Ball strategy carried over into the second half. We walked the ball up the court, passing back and forth, and back and forth, like we had all the time in the world. Because we did. The other team's attempts to steal ended more often than not with reach-in fouls. Their best players sat on the bench with foul trouble while we kept running our motion continuity offense. If we didn't have a layup or an open shot, we brought the ball back out and ran the continuity again. The girls were realizing that, though it seemed odd, though it went against every instinct to push the pace, we could adapt to the situation at hand.

Then came perhaps one of the funniest moments of my coaching career. The official made a call I vehemently questioned—a blocking foul that should have been a charge. Both my arms shot up in the air in exasperation, and I shouted, "What?!" Well, in my snap reaction to being frustrated, I'd completely forgotten I had two aluminum crutches propped under my arms. They both simultaneously fell away from my body and crashed toward the ground, hitting the wood floor with a resounding metallic CLANG- CLANG that echoed throughout the entire gym.

The gym went silent. Every head turned.

"Sorry!" I called out to everyone within earshot, mortified. "Sorry for that!" I bent down—awkwardly, painfully—and retrieved my crutches while my assistant coach covered her face, her shoulders shaking with laughter. I turned back toward the bench, not facing the court, and giggled with my players with crutches finally secure, while the game resumed behind me.

We won 34–31. A three-point victory that felt like winning a championship. As we shook hands with the Blair Academy team afterward, I could see the frustration still etched on their faces, but also a grudging respect. We'd found a way.

That day, we learned a lifelong lesson about adjusting to circumstances, being resilient when things don't go as planned, and embracing laughter—especially at ourselves. Sometimes the obstacle becomes the path forward. Sometimes an injury forces you to coach in a way you never would have chosen. And sometimes, the loudest sound in the gym is your crutches hitting the floor.

We still laugh about that game.

This story is one of many that shaped how I coached and how I lived. Over the years, I collected these moments—the ones that tested us, stretched us, made us dig deeper than we thought possible. They became the foundation of the pre-game speeches I'd give before every game, the stories I'd share when a player was doubting herself, the reminders I'd offer when life knocked someone down.

In this collection of pre-game speeches, you'll discover strategies for cultivating resilience and courage in the face of life's challenges. Each story serves as a powerful reminder that strength lies within us all—sometimes we just need someone else to believe in us and give us that firm nudge to get back in the game. Whether you're facing an overmatched opponent on a small court, nursing an injury that threatens to sideline you, or navigating any of life's unexpected obstacles, the lesson remains the same: adjust, be resilient, and never forget to laugh.

If You Meet a Bear in the Woods

It's going to be a tough game today. We are facing the undefeated team with the number one seed. That doesn't matter today. Today, we stand up tall and we play with confidence in all that we have accomplished and worked hard for this season. Today, we play the best that we can and do not back down.

Do you know what you should do if you meet a bear in the woods? And of course I hope you never will... Haha! You make yourself look big—stand tall, raise your arms, widen your stance, and jump up and down screaming!.

Don't make eye contact with the bear—they may see this as a threat or a challenge. Make loud noises—yell, clap your hands, use a bear bell, or bang things together. Then back away slowly—don't run, keep backing away until the bear is out of sight.

We must come out fighting from the tip till the final buzzer.

This is a lesson in bravery: When fear looms large, standing your ground with composure and courage can often turn the tide, allowing you to face challenges without letting panic take control.

We ultimately would lose this game—not because we backed down, but because the other team had more talent. The two-hour-and-forty-five-minute journey to Kimball Union Academy in New Hampshire had given me time to touch base with each player, let them listen to their pre-game music, and watch a movie. We were prepared for a fierce battle against the perennial champions. I've always held great respect for their coach, and when we cross paths, it's a warm and fond connection, built on years of competition and mutual admiration.

The game was neck and neck, coming down to the final minutes. A turnover here, a missed shot there, without those, we could've done it. For a moment, I truly believed we might pull off an upset. But as the clock wound down, a few missed opportunities tipped the scales, and the game slipped through our fingers. Though we didn't claim the win, we left knowing we had given everything, playing with heart and determination until the very end. We rose big against the bear.

It takes a strong resolve and courage to stand up and face whatever challenge you are facing head-on. Sometimes it is a difficult situation at work, or in your relationship, or with a family member. In each case, we have the tendency to handle these based on our inherent survival instincts: fight, flight, freeze, or fawn. As defined by WebMD, "The fight response is your body's way of facing any perceived threat aggressively. Flight means your body urges you to run from danger. Freeze is your body's inability to move or act against a threat. Fawn is your body's stress response to try to please someone to avoid conflict."

One crisp fall afternoon, my daughter and I set off on our favorite hiking trail in the mountains around Woodstock, Vermont. The path winds through thick forests, vibrant seasonal flowers, and around a serene pogue of water, rewarding hikers with a stunning panoramic view at the top. It's our tradition: At times, we will make it to the top of the two-and-a-half-mile journey and she will read or write in her journal, while I sit and enjoy the breathtaking views.

This time, however, the descent became an adventure of its own. As we marched down the trail, singing loudly, which we loved to do with no one else in sight, a sudden rustling in the brush ahead stopped us in our tracks. We froze for a beat, peering cautiously. A bear? No. A lot smaller—a big, fat, undeniably ugly porcupine.

Without thinking, we screamed and bolted back up the trail, hearts racing, unable to stop laughing at the absurdity of it all. A porcupine??? On the trail??? Who knew!!! Once we were safely out of porcupine range, whatever that might be, we turned to the ultimate authority on wildlife encounters: Google. I typed in: "What to do if you see a porcupine in the woods?" The advice was pretty straightforward and comforting: "Just steer clear. The very best thing you can do is keep your distance and respect their personal space. The rumor that porcupines can shoot or throw their quills is only a legend, but there's no need to test that out for yourself."

Relieved to learn we wouldn't be pelted with quills, we gathered our courage. Hiking poles in hand, we hugged the far edge of the trail away from the porcupine and sprinted past our spiky adversary. Phew.

The incident left me thinking. When facing a bear, the advice is to stand tall. Thankfully, I haven't had to test that theory! When facing a porcupine, the advice is to avoid and create distance. In each case, the metaphor applies: In life, standing tall for your beliefs—doing your research and presenting your case with confidence—is often the best approach. But there are times where a more cerebral tempered decision is needed. Whether it's porcupines on the trail or bears or challenges at work, courage, preparation, and resolve must be counted on to survive.

Hard Work Before Success

I still have it. It may be a few tenths of a second off, and there is a small crack in the glass face. I keep it in my jewelry box as one of my most valuable keepsakes. It is not worth anything to anyone but me. It is invaluable to me. The cold medal fits in half my palm, and the "tick, tick, tick" of each second resonates loudly in my ears.

It is my stopwatch that my parents gave me when I was in seventh grade.

I started running track in junior high. When I was in seventh grade, a ninth grader, Linda, was the fastest girl I ever saw. She was tall and lean. She ran the hurdles with grace like a gazelle. Her knees would clear the bar with barely an inch to spare. I never saw her lose a hurdle race.

Every day at the end of practice, our coach would have the sprinters end with a race. First the boys, then the girls. Linda and I would line up next to each other on the grass, trying to dig in our feet for traction at the start. (We didn't have a track until high school.) "On your mark... Get set... GO!"

At the end of the 100 yards stood the coaches with their stopwatches. "Click!" stopped the dial as we leaned to the finish line. Linda beat me by a nose each time. I would go home discouraged.

The next week was spring break, and that is when my dad bought me the stopwatch. He encouraged me to train on my own every day at the high school's track. Train, and I will be faster. Work hard, and I will get better. I owed it to myself.

I sprinted and sprinted, holding that stopwatch in my palm. And with each session, I saw improvement.

That first track practice after break, we stood again at the starting line ready to end the day with a race. "On your mark... Get set... GO!" At the finish line this time, I won. I won by a nose.

This pre-game message was straightforward: Put in the time, and the results will come. For me, it boiled down to a simple cause and effect. I wasn't competing with anyone else—I was doing it for myself. Sure, I could have accepted the reality that Linda was faster than I was from the start. But I owed it to myself to push, to test my limits, and to see what I was capable of achieving.

Linda and I would eventually run as teammates on the high school 4x100 relay team. We would reach the state championship finals and finish fifth. Thanks to my dad for buying me that stopwatch and challenging my resolve.

That said, sometimes life doesn't reward effort with the results we hope for. The paper you poured your heart into might still earn a B. The proposal that consumed weeks of late nights might still fail to secure the job. These disappointments are inevitable. However, the difference lies in the effort. If you give 100 percent, you can walk away knowing you left it all on the table. There's no shame in falling short when you've done your best. You learn, you adapt, and you move forward, stronger and more prepared for the next challenge.

Great quote:

"The only time success comes before work is in the dictionary."

—Vince Lombardi

When my friend Donna and I worked together at PrimoDonna Productions, we would meet in the morning, go for a run, work all day until late, sometimes work out again, and order in dinner, before I would leave to go home for the night. It was easy to work hard on our projects because we were good friends and both had the grit-and-grind mentality.

We launched PrimoDonna in 1988, just as the technology boom was gaining momentum. By 1989, we were presented with an incredible opportunity: Nynex Corporation, a major telecommunications company serving New England and New York, invited us to bid on a project for Ellis Island. At the time, the iconic site was undergoing extensive renovations as part of a large-scale restoration effort that began in the mid–1980s.

The Nynex executives took us to the construction site by tugboat, where we donned hard hats and explored the Great Hall. It was nothing but a shell—planks and dirt stretched across what would one day become a bustling historical landmark. As we walked through, they shared blueprints and their vision for the completed project. Our task? To design cutting-edge touchscreen technology to guide visitors through the newly envisioned historical museum.

Donna and I worked tirelessly on the proposal, meticulously aligning the latest technology with an engaging and intuitive user experience. When the time came, Donna delivered our vision with confidence and passion. However, despite our best efforts, we didn't win the bid.

Of course, we were deeply disappointed. But instead of dwelling on the loss, we recognized the value of the experience. It sharpened our skills, broadened our perspective, and prepared us for the next opportunity.

One setback wasn't the end. Rather, it was the process of our hard work that built the foundation for our future success.

Pivot or Push

What does 3:12 mean to you? One of my fondest coaching memories is a story about perseverance and never giving up that occurred in 2006.

We were 22-0 at the time of the New England Class A semi-final game. We were playing a team we had beaten by a few points twice before. And everyone knows how difficult it is in any sport to beat a team three times in a season.

But this game we did not play well. We found ourselves down by nine points with 3:12 to go. In the very, very far reaches of my mind, I thought, "It's OK. Not our day. 22-1 is a great record." WHAT???? GET RID OF THOSE THOUGHTS!! I KNEW IF I WAS THINKING THAT, SO WERE MY PLAYERS.

So...we had the ball at halfcourt and with 3:12 to go, I called a timeout.

As my team was running off the court, the other team was jumping up and down, cheering and relishing their nine-point lead.

In the huddle, I said very calmly, "Look at them. They think they won, but there is plenty of time. We got this. Three stops, Three scores. Pick them up full court, man, and box out. Rebound and run. We will run our sideline out of bound and play for a three. Then run it again with the second option until they stop it. I believe we got this."

We inbounded the ball... Executed the play to perfection...

And well, you know where this is going...

Without giving you the play-by-play (that will come later), we turned it around and rode our new momentum to finish on a 15-2 run and win by four. Greatest comeback ever!!! We will play to the final buzzer and believe together.

This is one of my all-time favorite pre-game speeches because its message is so universally powerful—it applies to nearly every aspect of life. In any challenge, you're often faced with two choices: Pivot and change your approach, or double down and keep going.

I often delivered this speech in those moments when we were up against a team with more talent, when I had that gut feeling we'd face a deficit and need to claw our way back. It wasn't about sugarcoating reality; it was about planting the seed of resilience.

One never knows the hurdles, the speed bumps, the obstacles, etc., that will come up in life. The challenge is not to allow them to stop you, but to adjust and keep going.

Visualize the stream flowing downhill in the woods. The water doesn't stop when it meets a rock; rather, it flows to one side and keeps going.

I was a big dreamer when I was growing up. I first wanted to be a professional tennis player. But I lived in New England, and indoor tennis lessons were cost-prohibitive. *Pivot.*

Then I wanted to be in the Olympics as a sprinter; I was fast, but not that fast. *Pivot.*

Then I dreamed of being on the Olympic women's basketball team. I was invited to Colorado Springs for the 1984 tryout but was not selected as one of the team's final roster. I did get the opportunity to represent the USA in the World Maccabiah Games. I won a silver medal as a player, a silver medal in the 4x400 relay, and five gold medals as a head coach. *Pivot.*

And finally, I wanted to be a sports broadcaster. I had the thrill of being a women's basketball analyst on ESPN, but I stepped away when my daughter was born and I got a divorce. *Pivot.*

Life's situations led me to find my true passion... Coaching.

Pushing through things that are hard means summoning your energy to keep going. This is something that takes guts and heart. Don't allow yourself to go down the rabbit hole of discouragement. Talk to yourself; don't listen to yourself. Use positive thoughts to propel you onward.

Here's a story that captures the perfect blend of pivot and push. When I was in junior high school, I was a sprinter on the track team. All season long, we raced on grass fields, and I competed in my trusty spikes with half-inch tips. Race after race, I came out on top. But everything changed at the citywide championship. The meet was being held at Newton North High School (NNHS), where they had just completed a state-of-the-art cork track.

As we warmed up, our coach gathered us and announced, "New track rules. Only one-quarter-inch spikes allowed." *What?!* I was stunned. How could they spring this on us now? I didn't have one-quarter-inch spikes, and my regular sneakers were bulky and would slow me down for sure. Panic set in. I had worked so hard all season, and now it felt like everything was unraveling in the big citywide championship.

My parents, who rarely missed a meet, saw my distress and rushed down to the track. Through tears, I explained the situation. They tried to brainstorm solutions—maybe they could run to a store and grab the right spikes? But time and distance weren't on our side. After a few minutes of deliberation with the coaches, we made a bold decision: I would run barefoot. It was unconventional, risky, and downright painful on that sunny eighty-plus-degree day with the scorching cork track, but it was the only way forward. *Pivot.*

Despite the odds, I ran the 100, the 220, and the 4x100 relay—barefoot—and I won them all. My feet were scorched and aching by the end of the day, but the victories were sweeter than ever. That moment taught me an invaluable lesson: Sometimes life throws you curveballs, and you have to adapt quickly. When you pivot with determination and push through the discomfort, you might just surprise yourself. *Pivot or push?*

No greater example of pushing forward in my life than battling breast cancer. Every day called for every ounce of my strength and fortitude. There was no other option than to keep going. *Push.*

People always ask how having cancer changed me. It first gave me the heightened perspective of not sweating the small stuff, keeping only those around me who are worth it. It also gave me full permission to exclaim, "When you find yourself going through hell... Keep going!"

Push.

Ride the Momentum

It's amazing the metaphors that driving can bring to life. I was in New York City, driving home on an early Sunday morning from visiting my daughter. I turned on 1st Avenue to stop at a red light at the next block. As far as my eye could see uptown, all the lights were a domino of red, until my light changed to green and all the lights followed.

Yes, I cruised the consecutive green lights. It was perfect, until it wasn't, and ten blocks up the light changed to red. I was stopped. However, I knew that it would change again to green, and I could once again begin my journey. One red light only stopped me for a brief moment in time. I had to wait to get going again.

The game is an ebb and flow. We will make a scoring run, then the other team can go on a run. The game isn't won in the first minute or after twenty or even in the thirty-first minute. It takes all 32 minutes. If we falter, get back up, figure it out, and push forward. We will play each play until the final buzzer.

Life often feels effortless when everything is going smoothly, but it's in the tough times that your true character is revealed. How do you respond when things don't go as planned? Who do you turn to for support? Where do you go to find your balance?

As part of my team bonding activities, I like to ask players what they do when they're frustrated. Many of them say they reach out to a friend, talk to their mom, or listen to music. Some say they play basketball, but that doesn't always work if basketball itself is the source of their stress. Personally, I've always found peace in walking along the beach or hiking in the mountains—activities that ground me and allow me to reset my thoughts.

A recent conversation with my daughter, Marcia, opened my eyes to the ways we recharge and cope differently. She explained that introverts thrive in solitude and feel recharged by quiet moments, while extroverts gain energy from socializing, enjoying the buzz of being around others. They're often gregarious, assertive, and adaptable.

As we discussed, we realized that most people don't fit neatly into one category or the other. Instead, we occupy a space somewhere between the two, adapting based on the situation. For instance, I've always thought of myself as shy during my childhood, yet that shyness disappeared when I stepped into the competitive arena or pursued my career, especially in broadcasting. The pressure of competition unlocked a boldness in me that might not have surfaced otherwise. Still, I've always needed solitude to recharge—quiet moments of reflection to regain my energy. I enjoy moments spent with myself.

This conversation led me to an important realization: We all need mechanisms—strategies, tools, or mindsets—to help us navigate life's inevitable challenges. The key is to develop these tools before you need them. Whether you're someone who finds strength in solitude or thrives in the energy of social connections, knowing what grounds you is essential.

Life will always throw obstacles your way. How you handle these obstacles is your response. By identifying what recharges you—whether it's a walk on the beach, a conversation with a trusted friend, or simply a quiet moment listening to music—you can face difficulties with resilience and clarity. Bumps and challenges are unavoidable, but when you have the right tools in place, you're better prepared to navigate them with confidence. By being mindful of what recharges you, you can face life's obstacles with greater resilience and clarity. So, pick one or many and don't hesitate to use them. Ride the positivity until another huddle and you take it out of your toolbox...again.

When I was a women's basketball broadcast analyst, there was nothing quite like the adrenaline rush of hearing the ESPN director in my earpiece say, "Thirty seconds to air." Standing on the court with the play-by-play announcer, the deafening roar of thousands of fans gearing up for the game was almost overwhelming. My focus would narrow to the camera operator in front of me, waiting for the director's cue: "We're LIVE." And just like that, the game—and the broadcast—was underway.

During my years as a broadcast analyst for women's basketball on ESPN, NESN, SportsChannel, Big East TV, and the Atlantic 10 Network, I had the privilege of traveling across the country to announce games. It was the perfect stage of life for such a whirlwind schedule—single and untethered, I could embrace the chaos and excitement of life on the road. From the charm of Des Moines, Iowa, to the glitz of Los Angeles, every city offered its own unique experiences.

One weekend epitomized this frenetic pace: I flew to Los Angeles to call a game between University of Southern California (USC) and Stanford. It was Hall of Famer Lisa Leslie's freshman year at USC, and Stanford was fresh off a national championship. After the game, I caught a red-eye back to New York and drove two hours through a snowstorm to UConn to cover a Big East showdown. These were exhausting but exhilarating days, and I relished every moment. Between 1988–1995, women's basketball games were not readily available on television, as they thankfully are now with the explosion of women's sports on air.

Broadcasting in the late '80s and early '90s came with its challenges and quirks. Updated game notes were faxed to our hotel rooms, and any breaking news was shared on-site, usually when we arrived at the arena a couple of hours before tip-off.

I had the privilege of working alongside some of the now-legends of broadcasting, including Robin Roberts, Mike Tirico, and Joe Buck. I'll never forget meeting Robin, in 1993 at a marquee game between UConn and Virginia in Storrs, CT. UConn, led by Geno Auriemma and Chris Dailey, had yet to solidify its place as a powerhouse, while Virginia, under Hall of Fame coach Debbie Ryan, was a perennial Final Four contender. Dawn Staley led them to three Final Fours and an NCAA tournament runner-up in 1991 before graduating in 1992, leaving big shoes to fill. Dawn went on to be a three-time Olympian and is currently the head coach of South Carolina, the three-time NCAA Division 1 National Champion. UConn was knocking at the door of significant postseason play but had not gotten past the Sweet Sixteen. Geno Auriemma and Chris Dailey had taken over in 1985. They are now the all-time winningest coaches in men's and women's basketball and together have led their teams to twelve national championships!

Robin was every bit the consummate professional—gracious, sharp, and down-to-earth. She joked that I'd have to "carry the broadcast," but it was a team effort in an electric Gampel Pavilion. UConn's 74-63 win that night felt like a turning point for their program, setting the stage for their dominance in the years to come. UConn's first NCAA Championship came on the heels of an undefeated year in 1995. Hall of Famer Rebecca Lobo led the way. Each home game that year, her grandmother would sit right behind the announcers' table, and we became acquaintances. She was so sweet and kind. I would share stats and stories with her. Each year, she would send me a Hanukkah card, and even one year, she made a small crochet Jewish Star ornament that I still have on my desk. Those were the connections that I valued most.

Announcing wasn't just a job—it was a masterclass in coaching. I had the rare opportunity to interview, observe, and analyze some of the greatest minds in women's basketball. From Pat Summitt's ferocious intensity at Tennessee to Muffet McGraw's tactical brilliance at Notre Dame, every game was a lesson.

One unforgettable moment came during a game between ranked number twenty Notre Dame and ranked number three Tennessee in 1991. It was a game Tennessee would eventually win 88-71. Thompson-Boling Arena would often sell out, and the crowd noise was deafening when the band belted out "Rocky Top." While the action on the court was captivating, I couldn't help but notice Pat Summitt and Muffet McGraw's baby boys with them post-game. It was a powerful image of balance and possibility—proof that women coaches could truly have it all.

The roster of coaches I had the privilege of interviewing and observing was nothing short of a "Who's Who" in women's basketball. Pat Summit was the most professional and welcoming person, and as intimidating and intense as she would appear on the sidelines, she always made me feel at ease. We would even joke about where we bought our suits. Andy Landers, the longtime head coach at Georgia; Bonnie Henrickson, who made her mark at Virginia Tech, Kansas, and University of California, Santa Barbara; C. Vivian Stringer, a legend at Iowa and Rutgers; and Tara VanDerveer, the iconic Stanford coach.

Others on this extraordinary list include Ohio State's Jim Foster, Louisiana Tech's Leon Barmore and Kim Mulkey, St. Joseph's Stephanie Gaitley, and Virginia's Debbie Ryan. Dawn Staley first started at Temple University before making history at South Carolina. At the time, I didn't fully grasp the significance of these experiences. But in retrospect, my role as a broadcaster gave me a unique lens into the art and science of coaching. Observing these remarkable leaders in action and hearing their insights shaped my understanding of the game, deepening my appreciation for strategy, leadership, and teaching in ways I only came to value fully later on.

But when my daughter was born in 1996, my priorities shifted. By 1997, I made the difficult decision to step away from broadcasting to focus on raising her as a single mom going through a divorce. While it was bittersweet to leave the road and the mic behind, this transition opened the door to a new chapter: coaching.

Looking back, I realize how much my years as a broadcast analyst prepared me for this next step. Watching practices, interviewing coaches, and analyzing games gave me unparalleled insight into the game's strategies and nuances. The lessons I learned from the legends in the game continue to shape my approach to this day.

Broadcasting was an extraordinary chapter in my life—a front-row seat to history and a hands-on education in excellence. Though the road took me in a new direction, I carry those experiences with me, grateful for the journey, the ride of momentum, and the foundation it laid for what came next.

Attitude & Effort

Two things a coach should never have to teach are attitude and effort. These are the foundational qualities every player should bring with them—showing up with a positive mindset, high energy, and giving their best effort at all times. These traits shouldn't be seen as exceptional or praiseworthy; they should be the baseline expectation. A strong team culture begins with everyone holding themselves accountable for these fundamentals.

Being a coach, a boss, or a leader involves many factors to account for if you want people to follow your vision. Organizing people to collaborate on a mission is difficult enough, but nearly impossible if people show up with low energy and bad attitudes. Many things in life are not in one's control; attitude and energy are not among them. How you show up to work or play on the court, every time, is all in YOUR power.

My athletic director once gave a lecture to the girls at a basketball camp I was running. I will always remember when he said, "You can't fool the person in the mirror." Think about that quote. You can probably fool most people into thinking you are working hard, or did what you could, but you can't fool yourself!

Marcia and I make a dynamic mother-daughter duo, strengthened by the love and support of family and friends. My parents lived right next door, showering her with the unconditional love only grandparents can give, while my sister and her family were just a few miles away, always present to enrich our lives. My friends embraced Marcia as part of our circle, understanding when she joined me at meetings or even at Super Bowl parties. My Aunt Margie's timeless advice—give your child "love and wings"—became a guiding principle. Even through the challenges of a divorce and navigating visitation, Marcia grew into a grounded and well-adjusted person. I credit this to parenting with patience, guidance, and a deep, unwavering love. I created space for her to blossom into her authentic self.

Our joy was rooted in the simple, meaningful moments we spent together. It didn't matter where or what we were doing. We were fortunate to explore places like Niagara Falls, the Grand Canyon, Oxford, England, Brazil, Israel, Italy, the Cayman Islands, Vermont, Maine, New York City, and San Diego, as well as countless cities along the New England seaboard. Going to Broadway musicals, museums, aquariums, professional sporting events, and more is all part of our adventures. Hiking in the mountains became a cherished pastime, filled with adventure and laughter. The closeness of our relationship was often admired by both her friends and mine, becoming a hallmark of our bond. And when delays happened and things didn't go as planned, we approached them with a positive lens and a good attitude. So many small, seemingly insignificant moments were turned into laughs and lifetime memories.

During my tenure as athletic director at Marcia's school, we commuted together daily. Our car rides became opportunities for deep conversations that went far beyond the surface-level "How was school?" and "Fine." Instead, we debated topics like assembly speakers or dissected the social dynamics of the school cafeteria. After school, Marcia would sit in my office doing her homework while I coached or worked late until she went to crew practice. These shared moments became the fabric of our daily lives, stitching us closer together. I was lucky to have chosen a profession that my daughter could be with me when needed.

Marcia's artistic and singing journey added a beautiful dimension to our lives. In elementary school she was always one of the leads in her school plays, such as the Lion in The Wizard of Oz, Ms. Hanigan in *Annie*, and the Baroness in *The Sound of Music*. Her voice was beautiful, and she was chosen to be part of the Boston City Singers (BCS), a prestigious youth choir that celebrated diversity and inspired excellence in music. Every Tuesday evening, we drove to Dorchester for rehearsals. While she sang, I sat in the adjacent room, savoring the harmony they created. Unlike the competitive nature of athletics—where outcomes were black and white, win or lose—music was about harmony and balance. Of course, on your own team, lessons of harmony had to be taught and cultivated, but in competition, it was win or lose.

The choir's artistic director and I often discussed the joy of watching these kids create something bigger than themselves, each carrying their weight to weave a beautiful musical tapestry. My eight years of playing the clarinet had given me an appreciation of music, and since this was Marcia's pursuit, I appreciated music even more and supported her efforts.

In the summer of 2009, the choir traveled to Newfoundland and Labrador, Canada, to participate in Festival 500, a renowned international choral festival. I was honored to be one of the chaperones, and my coaching background proved invaluable in keeping the thirty-plus teenagers organized and disciplined. Sharing this extraordinary experience with Marcia was a special gift.

The people of Newfoundland welcomed us warmly, and the performances were nothing short of angelic. The singers gave their all, pouring their hearts into rehearsals and concerts. Each note resonated with the positive energy and dedication they brought, creating an atmosphere of pure magic. This trip remains one of the most memorable adventures Marcia and I have shared, a beautiful chapter in the story of our mother-daughter bond.

I realized that whether in sports, academics, music, business, or relationships, the common thread for achieving success lies in bringing a positive attitude and putting forth genuine effort.

If a Video Camera Followed You All Day, What Would It Record?

> *Think about your every action on and off the court. When you run out for warm-ups, are you focused or looking in the stands for your parents? When your teammate makes a bad pass, how do you react? And when you miss an open layup, do you put your head down and get discouraged? And when you come to the bench, are you pissed off or do you stop and listen to me?*
>
> *Now imagine there is a camera recording your every move. How would your actions change?*
>
> *I want you to pretend that is the case to flip the narrative and make it all positive. Be a supportive teammate. Be focused every play, regardless of who is in the stands. Turn a failure into a lesson. And be open to coaching; it will help make you a better player. Go to the next play and do it with a smile!*

Now, picture that imaginary camera on your shoulder, following you throughout the day. It's there, recording every moment, every decision, and every interaction. At the end of the day, when you rewind the footage and watch it play back, what would you see? Would you be happy with what you've done? Would your boss, your coworkers, your friends, or your family members be proud of the way you carried yourself?

Let's think about it. How do you begin your day? Do you hold the door for the person behind you as you enter the building, offering a simple gesture of courtesy? Do you take the extra moment to smile or greet someone, brightening their day with just a few kind words? Even if they don't comment in response, that smile or greeting might be exactly what they needed at that moment.

As you move through your day, how do you spend your time? Are you focused on your tasks, or are you occasionally distracted by your phone and scrolling through social media or playing games? What if you made a conscious decision to put the phone down for those few extra hours and instead focused fully on your work, helping your team meet deadlines and moving the project forward? Imagine the satisfaction of finishing your tasks early or efficiently and having time to assist someone else who might be struggling.

Do you ever stay late to finish up a report or meet a deadline, not because anyone's asking you to, but because you know it's important, and you care about the quality of your work? Imagine the appreciation from your boss when they notice your dedication. That you're going above and beyond, ensuring that your contributions are valued and impactful.

Later in the day, do you stop at the market for a family member who is unable to go, even though it's the last thing you'd want to do after a long day? Perhaps you don't mind the small inconvenience, because you know it will ease their burden and make them feel supported. A simple errand can create a sense of connection, showing that you care enough to make their life a little easier.

Now, imagine that all of these seemingly small, yet significant moments, were captured on that camera. These actions don't always get noticed or rewarded, nor edited into a highlight video, but when we stop and think about them, they add up. Your small acts of kindness, your extra effort, your willingness to step outside of yourself for others—these moments have ripple effects. Maybe your coworker, who is feeling overwhelmed by the workload, is quietly grateful for your help. Or your friend who is going through a tough time feels a little lighter because you took a moment to reach out.

If you could see this footage at the end of the day, how would it make you feel? Would you be proud of the energy and intention you put into the world? Would you realize that all those little choices made a big difference—not just for you, but for everyone around you?

When we live knowing that every action matters, we begin to see life not as a series of tasks to get through, but as an opportunity to be our best selves in the world. Now, with this mindset, when you rewind your day in your mind, ask yourself: What will the camera show?

In 1989, Donna and I were hired to create a highlight video for the USA VIP sponsors of the Maccabiah Games. Two years previously, we had launched a video production company called PrimoDonna Productions—a playful nod to the term "prima donna," reflecting both our personalities and our vision. Having both competed in the Maccabiah Games years prior, being on the board, and knowing many people in the organization, we felt confident that we could craft an inspiring and impactful video that would encapsulate the essence of the USA VIPs' three-week journey.

We set out to produce a memorable video by pre-recording a voiceover by the renowned Norman Rose and selecting music tracks that included Whitney Houston's iconic song, "One Moment in Time." We meticulously planned every detail, from the shots we hoped to capture to the narrative structure we wanted to craft. Each day, we worked closely with an Israeli camera crew, filming a variety of moments ranging from the excitement of sporting events to scenic tours of Israel. We visited the Western Wall in Jerusalem, climbed Masada, floated in the Dead Sea, and captured the grandeur of the opening ceremony. The pomp and circumstance of bringing together thousands of Jewish athletes from seventy-five countries to compete in an international competition was a sight to behold. Russian Jewish athletes were able to compete for the first time in the history of the games.

Once all the footage was shot, the real work began: the editing. We hired an editor who, though limited in English, had an extraordinary eye for crafting compelling narratives. Hour after hour, shot by shot, we painstakingly chose the perfect sequences to create a seamless, beautiful story. Although we knew that the VIPs watching the video wouldn't fully grasp the precise effort we were putting into every cut and transition, we were doing this for ourselves as much as for them. We wanted this video to be something we could be proud of, something that truly reflected the dedication and spirit of the games.

For thirty-six straight hours, we edited. Lying on the floor, up in a chair, and sometimes arguing with our Israeli editor, we trimmed, rearranged, refined, and polished frame by frame. We would pick up food and eat it as we edited. By the time we finished the final cut, we were exhausted but eager to see the fruits of our labor come to life.

We took the completed tape and arranged a car to transport us the two-hour drive from Tel Aviv to Jerusalem. As Donna and I stood in the back of the ballroom, arm in arm, watching the video play for the crowd of over a thousand VIPs, we were overwhelmed. The footage we had captured—the athletic feats, the emotional moments, and the sheer beauty of the experience—was now unfolding before the very people we had worked so tirelessly for.

Exhausted but exhilarated, tears filled our eyes as we shared in the collective emotion of the crowd. The VIPs watched in awe, seeing their incredible journey play out on the screen in front of them. What our camera recorded wasn't just a series of images—it captured the effort, the dedication, and the love that Donna and I poured into making sure that our video would leave a lasting impression on everyone who experienced it. This video is still my all-time favorite.

It wasn't about the technical perfection of each edit or the fame of the people involved; it was about the impact of those final moments, when the video came to life and brought us all together in a shared emotional experience. That's what we had worked for, and that's what we had created—a lasting memory, beautifully captured.

FOURTH QUARTER

Believe

We are constantly surrounded by quotes, stories, and shows about the power of belief. I'll admit, there are days when I shake my head and think, *Not today*. But then, there are those moments when the act of believing resonates deeply, striking a chord in my soul. In those moments, I smile knowing I can have a shot and in the end say: "Yes, I did believe."

This is the spirit I always try to channel in my pre-game speeches. I want my players to reach deep within themselves, to find that spark of belief—not just in winning, making shots, or playing tough defense—but to see how these moments are connected to something greater than the game itself. Belief is what transforms effort into possibility and turns ordinary actions into something extraordinary.

3:12 to go...

What does three minutes and twelve seconds mean to you?

What can you accomplish with that amount of time?

Not very much... or .... everything.

Seriously, what can you accomplish within three minutes and twelve seconds? Eat? Quickly. Drink a cup of coffee? Gulp it down. Drive through for fast food? Definitely not. Watch a show on Netflix? Only a tease. Workout? Wouldn't even break a sweat.

And chances are, three minutes and twelve seconds have already passed since you were reading this.

For me, one assistant coach, twelve players, one daughter, countless parents, and fans, 3:12 changed our collective lives. My 3:12 just happened to be played out in a basketball game, but this digression and recount of a singular event will help realize that my mentality to fight cancer was driven by my past. A life of big dreams manifested itself in accomplishing the biggest dream of all: living.

In the 2006 New England Class A Championship semi-final game with 3:12 remaining, trailing by nine points, 38-47, I called a timeout with the ball at halfcourt. Anyone who has ever played or watched a game of girls' high school basketball would know that for a team to be down by nine points with only 3:12 on the clock, would say that those are insurmountable odds to make a comeback. I agree, but successful dreams are rooted in a bit of reality, and coming back to complete an undefeated season was maybe a probable NO or a possible YES.

To give you some context, parents are not supposed to have a favorite child, but a coach can have a favorite team. Perks of being a coach! The chemistry of the players in this particular team, the individuals involved, the depth of the journey, and the hardships we overcame together as a team changed my life forever. The starting five: Laticia and Gisemi; Alicia, a junior whose father was suffering from the debilitating, incurable disease of ALS; Roshonda, who was the younger sister of Freddie, who was born with Down syndrome and given a month to live. Sweet Freddie was seventeen, and his mom drove him to every game in her big green accessible van; and Sara, a post-graduate who earned her Division I scholarship to Siena. She was the piece that we needed to put us over the top. And of course, me. A single mom going through a divorce.

When one talks about resilience and perseverance, you don't have to look further than this tapestry of players. They were from all different backgrounds, all with different baggage, and yet when we walked into the locker room and onto the court, we found a way to put our differences aside and compete. Compete for each other, and at times, forget what was going on outside of the court. It's a gift I have been given in much of my life: the ability to compartmentalize. To deal with the issue right in front of my nose and allow myself to enjoy the moment. To dream big and allow my mind to wander past the hardships and thrive in the possibilities.

Back to the game...

We were undefeated after winning twenty-two straight games, and were now playing a team we had beaten twice already during the season. At that moment, to the onlooker, it appeared that our beautiful, challenging, and memorable journey would not have the storybook ending we had so desired. But to us, as we watched the other team jump up and down jubilantly as they went to their bench for my called timeout, we believed it wasn't over. In my announcer's matter-of-fact, analytical voice, "We have three possessions. One stop at a time. Plenty of clock left." Ah, yes, cliché comments from an experienced coach.

I then drew up the first play: 10-:15, it takes ten to fifteen seconds to run it. This time it took ten seconds to run it, and Laticia was fouled while taking a three-pointer! And so it began... One free throw was made and the score was now 39-47. The pressure was on-ball defense and a turnover out of character from New Hampton's guard along the sideline. With the ball back, I figured we should run our three-point play again...

"Run 10-:15 again!" I yelled.

We started to, but Roshonda, our undersized post, was open on the block, and she received a beautiful pass from Gisemi and scored. We were now down by six, 41-47, with 2:41 to go.

I will pause here. Take a moment and ask yourself, How do you handle adversity? What do you do when something does NOT go as planned? When you are in the middle of doing something—anything, from homework to a test to a business proposal or a medical diagnosis—what is your mentality? THERE IS ALWAYS A WAY. You just need to be open to looking for it. It may take time. Sometimes, in fact, more time than you thought or hoped. Finding a positive opening. Not allowing the moment to take over and knock you out. If it knocks you down, get back in there. While there is time remaining, there is always a chance.

New Hampton came down on offense, ran a play, took a shot, missed. In the scramble for the loose ball, bodies go diving on the floor in a long trail to the sideline. Gisemi, all 5'3" of her, lies out in full extension. But

New Hampton's 6'3 girl with an extra foot ends up touching the ball last. I never thought I'd be that happy with a foot deficit in height.

This game was not Gisemi's best as she shot zero for six in three-point shots up to that point. But we had a special trusting relationship, and I believed in her. "Keep shooting," I always say, so we ran a play for Gisemi to get an open shot. She took it. She hit it! A three from the top of the key. We were now down by three, 44-47, with 1:58 on the clock.

Never quit. You hear those two words in almost everything you do. From teachers, coaches, colleagues, bosses, and motivational speakers... Why do you think that is so? Well, because it is true. If you stop. If you quit. If you give up. Then you lose. Trying and failing are totally separate ideals.

You cannot be successful at everything you take on. As long as you keep trying, you will keep failing. But that is OK. Failure in and of itself is part of life. What you do with failure is the key. Failure is your best teacher. Look at what you can learn? And then, keep on going. I have a poster in my room that reads, "Opportunity... You will always miss 100% of the shots you do not take." It doesn't always mean you will succeed, but at least there is hope if you try.

Back to the game...

My best defender, Laticia, became the heroine of our story. Something inside her was ignited, and her tenacity took over. Laticia would go on to earn a D2 scholarship. She would blow out her knee, which stalled her basketball career, but like Gisemi, she had an inner resilience to move forward. Laticia is beautiful inside and out, and always was a bright light. She is now a successful model, actress, and entrepreneur.

Laticia steals the ball clean at midcourt, then drives to the basket. She gets bumped, ball up, fouled, scores, and we're now one way! The score is tied 47-47 with 1:43 to go. New Hampton is now stunned. They were no longer jumping up and down with excitement. Instead, our fans were exuberant. There's a quote, "If you want a happy ending, it depends on when you stop the story." The ending to this game was yet to be written. Another time out, and this time it was taken by them.

I often wonder if my 3:12 story of believing has defined so much of how I think of challenges in my life. But what on earth do the members of

New Hampton think? Are our heroics equal to their collapse? Perhaps they look at it as the lesson of bouncing back from adversity after their defeat?

Why do athletic events polarize moments that seem bigger than life? Because the event is on display for all to see. Raw emotions, deep to the core, are felt by those participating and those watching. The focus of the moment for us was all that existed. This was not a one-person charge. This was a team brigade.

Facing insurmountable odds alone, well, is daunting. Downright hopeless. With others, the odds seem possible. In the timeout, I pointed to my heart and said, "This is where you will win this game."

My daughter chose rowing as her sport. She eventually got me hooked. The synchronization of eight people in a boat, rowing to the same rhythm, pulling with equally measured strokes, is truly the most beautiful display of teamwork. Relying on help, asking for assistance, drawing energy from friends, family, teammates, teachers, colleagues are all part of the equation to get through difficult times.

Be the best version of yourself. This sounds simple, but sometimes being your best isn't always the best. Working hard is a prerequisite for any level of success, but it's not the only thing. Many times people say, "But I studied so hard," "But I worked all night," "But I gave it my best." As you should. You should work hard. The problem is that hard work does not always translate into the results you hope for. But don't give up. Sometimes you have to shift your perspective. Sometimes you have to take a different path. Sometimes you have to change your expectations. And even sometimes, you have to change the game.

Sports are the ultimate showdown... Mano a mano... Carpe diem... Si se puede... Black and white... Win or lose... Hero and, well, not. Unfortunately, daily life is never this clear. It can take years to decipher what is clear or the reasons why.

A nine-point deficit with 3:12 to go in girls' high school basketball is a big hurdle. But in life, unfortunately, many of us face much bigger hurdles, greater tragedies, and profoundly deeper grief. This is where my breast cancer narrative fits in. Deeply ingrained in my personality, my persona, my psyche, is 3:12. Breast cancer was a path I never, ever expected, but when it reared its ugly head, I took it head-on. It was a path I did not survive on my own. I was humbled by the support and outreach. Cancer would not defeat me. I believed that I would defeat this. I believed that I would walk among my colleagues and they would not even be aware that I was going through chemo treatments. I hid the horrors that my body was experiencing under the wig I wore that looked like I just had my hair done at the beauty parlor; every day it looked that way. Day after day.

I shared my diagnosis with only a few close to me who would know the truth of my struggle. I worked when I could, and coached even if I could not stand. People asked me why I didn't take time off. My only logical response was that that is who I am. That was all that I knew. I am lucky. I am here telling you my story. This is my path. At the hospital one day, waiting for an appointment to schedule my radiation, I saw a little blond boy dressed in his jammies, holding hands with his parents. He could not be more than five years old. His mom was carrying a drinking cup with a straw when they stopped because the little boy asked for a sip. It was clear that this adorable little boy was going through cancer treatments, yet, as he walked along, he smiled and laughed. At that moment, he was my hero. He will never know that in a brief moment, he inspired me. Never be afraid of asking for help. Show resilience, be vulnerable to ask for help, and please be grateful for those who do.

An amazing phenomenon happened when I had gotten laryngitis each time from the chemo treatments. I believed that my team could understand me better when I couldn't speak. I know, I know, sounds silly. But they knew my hand signals and had to really focus on my expressions. My assistant, Caleigh Crowell, another of my former players at Worcester Academy, was a godsend in getting me through every day. We would make up poster boards with the plays that she would hold up, and I would whisper to her something that she and the girls would echo. After the game, the team understood that my energy was spent. Rather than head to the locker room for my post-game thoughts, they would sit in a circle around me on the court.

Greatest lesson of all: You can't go it alone. As a coach, I chuckle when I see my players on the court glance over to their parents in the stands. Part of me wants to yell, "No! Over here! I am the one you need to listen to." But then

I remember that I knew exactly where my dad was during all my games. My mom, on the other hand, was peering through the glass doors because she was too nervous to watch. That glance over provides support. If even for a few brief seconds, support from an approving nod or a clenched fist. Or simply reassurance that all will be OK. Family members, friends, teachers, coaches—it doesn't matter who. All that matters is that it is someone.

Another strip of the ball from their guard at half court led to another transition layup. We were now up 49-47 with 1:33 to go. After a foul on our part and a missed free throw on their part, we secured the defensive rebound, dribbled up the floor, made a long pass, and scored. It was now 51-47 with under a minute left in our historical comeback.

In moments like these, the clock seems to stand still... It could not go by quickly enough. Finally, they fouled us, and we made one; 52-47. They then scored to narrow the gap to 52-49. Yet it was still a one possession game with twenty-four seconds to go. Gisemi dribbled around, eluding the defense, passed it ahead to Rashonda at midcourt, who quickly relayed the ball to Alicia standing under the hoop. Alicia laid it in, was fouled, and that was essentially game over. We won! EPIC.

I imagine you are pretty confident that I would not tell you about 3:12 and our astounding comeback if we hadn't won. You would be correct. Alicia made the free throw, which she has since said was the most nervous she had ever been shooting a free throw. 3:12 changed our lives.

Ever been afraid? Doubtful? I don't mean the kind of afraid when you see the big hairy spider crawl near your feet or the afraid when you leave a chilling movie and you swear you heard something rustle in the bushes. No, I am talking about the afraid that gets you in the gut. Failure is scary. Letting people down is scary. However, fear can be the great motivator rather than the great crippler. How could we win twenty-two games only to lose now? It just wasn't an option. We took it head-on. Embraced our fear, accepted our fear. And attacked one play at a time. We believed.

The Fourth Quarter brings Pre-Game home with more meaningful speeches that cut straight to the heart of belief. That fire in your chest, that voice in your head saying "You've got this," it's everything. And the best part? You can build it, strengthen it, feed it. Believe.

Chance Favors Those
Who Are Prepared

> *We are ready. We worked really hard to prepare for this game. Our resolve to be our best and determination to work hard will give us the best chance to succeed. Practice is like eating your vegetables; the game is your dessert!*
>
> *There is no luck involved. We can control our destiny based on just how hard we prepared for this game. We can win the 50/50 battles. We can box back even though we are undersized. We can defend with all the energy and intensity we have worked on. Now, let's execute our offense and share the ball, and the ball will bounce our way because we are prepared.*
>
> *Let's go out and play like we practiced! Play smart. Play hard. Run, run, run, and have fun!*

When I played at Holy Cross from 1980–84, there were many memorable moments that I cherish on and off the court. Those years were more than just a chapter in my basketball career—they became the foundation for countless lessons and stories that now inspire my pre-game speeches. Each moment, from the thrill of victory to the challenges of defeat, to locker room speeches and practices, has woven itself into the fabric of my positive mindset, shaping how I approach life, and I now share that perspective with others.

I remember once when Togo briefly left the gym and returned moments later with a chair. He placed it down at midcourt and boldly declared, "Ladies, I have all night!" We had been practicing with far too little energy and focus, especially given that we were set to face our biggest rival, Boston College (BC), the next day. Our schools had a long-standing battle to claim the title of the top Jesuit program in the Northeast. I'd like to think that legends like Bob Cousy, Tom Heinsohn, and Togo Palazzi himself gave us a clear advantage!

"Play like you practice," Togo would remind us. In 1983, the NCAA didn't have the practice time restrictions it does today—or at least none that I can recall—so when Togo said he had all night, we knew he meant it. We quivered at the thought. For the next four hours, we ran, competed, and battled each other relentlessly. If anyone had evening plans, they were long forgotten; we were too exhausted to think of anything else.

We hardly ever lost at home. In fact, over my four years, our home record was 45-1. This game, like so many others, was a back-and-forth battle, with no team ever pulling ahead by more than a few points. It would come down to the final moments of the game to decide a winner.

To give some context, my college career was played before the three-point line existed, and we used a men's basketball. With just ten seconds left on the clock, we were down by one and had no choice but to foul BC's guard. If she made both free throws, the game was over. If she missed one, we'd still have a chance to make a bucket to send the game to overtime.

She stood at the line, went through her routine, and shot. The ball hit the back of the rim, bounced straight up, and struck the safety wire that holds the backboard to the stanchion—a violation. The ball miraculously was ours.

During the timeout, the play was drawn up for me to take the final shot. Somehow, I got free on the inbounds pass, grabbed the ball, and sprinted as fast as I could, weaving through defenders. I then stopped at the elbow and took the shot. I felt contact, but the officials didn't blow their whistles. My shot circled the rim and bounced out toward the opposite baseline.

In what felt like slow motion, the ball caromed perfectly into the hands of our freshman point guard, Karen. Off-balance and under pressure, Karen threw up a shot, and this time she clearly was fouled. The whistle rang out with one second remaining on the clock.

BC called a timeout, likely hoping to rattle Karen. In the huddle, Togo held his rosary beads. When we returned to the floor, Karen was calm. I, on the other hand, stood in the second rebound spot with the desperation of a potential rebound, bent over with hands on my knees, completely spent. The thought of overtime was just not an option.

Karen stepped to the line, took the ball from the official, and sank the first free throw to tie the game. *Send us home,* I thought as her second shot left her hands.

Swish!

We won! As the final buzzer sounded, I glanced over at the bench and saw my teammates elated, leaping into the air, and wrapping each other in celebration. Meanwhile, I stood at midcourt, still with my hands on my knees, every ounce of energy drained. I couldn't jump or cheer, but inside, I was soaring, overwhelmed with exhaustion and pure, unfiltered joy.

That game taught me something I've carried with me ever since: You never know when the next challenge is going to stare you down. Being prepared is hard work, but showing up every day and striving to be the best version of yourself means that when your moment comes, you'll be ready. And if it's not your moment in time, another will come. The key is to keep showing up, keep working, and keep believing.

Sand Castles Wash Away...

> *I hope you have had the opportunity to feel the grains of sand wash between your toes while the tide rushes in and out. Then, with the help of friends and family, carry buckets of sand to build castles, and dig holes deep enough for sitting in.*
>
> *It's something that you can spend hours building by first staking out your perfect spot, then walking back and forth to the water to dig for wet sand to pack your bucket, and finally constructing the foundation. When it's done, you look at your amazing work and take pictures standing over your newly built castle.*
>
> *But then, as with every day, the sun sets, the moon rises, and the tide comes in to wash away your sand castle. It's all part of the game. You make a great play, but you cannot be satisfied with that; you have to start over to do it again.*
>
> *Similarly, you make a mistake, start over, and go on to the next play.*

This metaphor captures the delicate nature of life and the constant opportunity for renewal. Life, much like the ocean, moves in cycles—the ebb and flow, the rise and fall, the shifting winds. It reflects the unpredictable rhythms of our daily existence.

In the reality of our everyday lives, some days will feel lighter than others. Some months will shine brighter, and some years will feel more challenging than others. But the key is in recognizing that this, too, shall pass. Just like the waves that gradually wash away a sandcastle, difficult moments will eventually recede. Embracing this truth empowers you to face the present with resilience and move forward, knowing that change is inevitable and growth is always possible.

There is no more nerve-racking or satisfying pre-game speech than the ones I've delivered before a championship or gold medal game. I once heard that coaching is an art, not a science. While certain game situations require knowledge and strategy, reading the room, taking the temperature of a team in the locker room before the final game, are things that come from the heart.

In major life events, too, sometimes no big rousing speech is needed. Often, saying nothing at all can speak volumes and set the stage. The players know what's at stake. All that's needed is a quiet reminder of our expectations and the strategy ahead, which often proves to be the most memorable.

In 2022, I had the privilege of coaching ten incredible women for the USA Open Women's Basketball team at the twenty-second World Maccabiah Games in Israel. This was a rare and special group, united by a singular goal: winning the gold medal. Every player checked their ego at the door, and we spent three unforgettable weeks together, fighting for a common purpose and immersing ourselves in our Jewish heritage.

Our journey began in a pre-camp in Princeton, New Jersey. For two days, we bonded on and off the court. We were led by Abby, the eventual MVP, who was an absolute joy to coach. A leader both on and off the court, Abby had just graduated from Princeton and was preparing to attend Maryland for her fifth year. She was never satisfied with her game—if she missed a few shots, she'd be out on the outdoor courts under the scorching Israeli sun, working on her jump shot. Abby had a tremendous work ethic and a mentor to the younger players.

Tess, another Ivy League player, had just graduated from Harvard and was preparing to play her fifth year at UC Davis, and Adara, who had played for me at Worcester Academy. We'd traveled together to St. Thomas, Budapest, and now Israel. Adara was our fearless point guard—she led us at Worcester Academy to two New England championships and two gold medals at the USA Maccabi Games.

Jamie was one of our strongest physical players, who, after graduating from Lehigh University, went to NYU, for her master's. Jamie was a member of their second national championship.

And Maddie, a Princeton and Davidson player, brought maturity and a deep love for the game. These five women were the starters and steady force that carried us forward.

Amit was our fiery Israeli American, Jaquelyn, our tallest player who could dunk a tennis ball, Sophie, a tall, lanky guard with excellent shooting touch, and who also played for me in Budapest, Molly played at Emory, and finally, Nina, who joined us from the three-on-three team and went on to play at Bryant University. My assistant coach was Monica Armstrong who was instrumental in our success, and the best team manager ever was my daughter, Marcia.

The gold medal game was scheduled to take place in the grand arena in Jerusalem. We gathered in the hotel lobby for a team photo before boarding the bus to the game. As we made our way through the bustling streets, weaving between traffic and passing ancient landmarks like the Old Wall outside the Temple Mount, alongside modern rails and highways, the anticipation in the air was palpable. Yet, amid this journey, my focus was shattered by a message I had received from my beloved Coach Togo's daughter, Mary Ann, telling me that Togo might not survive the week.

As the words sank in, I began to tear up. Marcia noticed, and I showed her the message. She held my hand, silently understanding that I couldn't talk about this news if I was to get through the game. I had to show up and be the best coach I could be. I tucked the news away, compartmentalized it, and focused on the task at hand.

The locker room was newly built, and the team sat in front of the lockers, lacing up their shoes and donning their USA uniforms. As I took a moment to gather myself, my heart was full. Full of gratitude for the opportunity to compete in this gold medal game with such a loving group of players, and for having my daughter share this moment with me. In the back of my mind, I thought of my dad in heaven, knowing how proud he would be of me. But above all, I wanted to win this for Togo.

Unlike the hundreds of pre-game speeches I have given that were not recorded, Marcia recorded this one. This is exactly what I said:

So, here we are in the nice locker room, the big arena, ready to play the game that you have worked so hard for. You don't need the big rousing speech. This is the gold medal game, you all know it. Everything you've worked for, everything you've done, leads to this moment. You show up today doing what you can do; doing what you can do, what you have worked so hard to do, and you bring it home. Five minutes at a time, whether it's the "Diamond or the Pencil," whether it's the "One Degree," whether it's the "Pebble" that makes each other better, the "Sticks" that make you stronger together, you all are doing what you need to do in this peak game. Right! We're going to peak today. It will be fun. We will do this together.

I have been fortunate in my career of non-coaching to be in the presence of a lot of amazing people, and one of them was Shonda Rhimes. And Shonda said, and I will never forget this, I immediately wrote it down... "We are all the main characters in our own story."

Every one of you, including me, the coach, including Marcia, including Summer, our team trainer, has a story. And the story that you choose to tell is in your power, is in your capabilities, and today, ladies, that story you can write is part of history.

Let's have some fun. Let's do it together. Let's peak today. Let's do what we set out to do over a year ago.

Win the gold medal.

Let's GOOOOOOOO!

We went on to win the gold medal in a commanding victory over the Israeli team—a game in which we truly did peak. As the final buzzer sounded and the scoreboard flashed 00:00, I was overcome with emotion and began to cry. Remember, I am a crier… Marcia and I embraced as our team rushed onto the court, gathering in a jubilant group hug, jumping up and down as confetti rained down from the rafters. My tears were a mix of joy for our triumph, knowing my dad was watching from heaven with pride, and an aching sadness, knowing that my mentor—my coach—was fighting for his life. The joy I experienced with this amazing group of players was something I carry with me each and every day.

I made it home just in time to visit Togo in the hospital with the gold medal in hand to show him. Two weeks later, he passed away.

Just like the waves that gradually wash away a sandcastle, difficult moments will eventually recede. The heartache of losing someone you love can feel like an overwhelming tide, relentless and consuming, while the joy of achieving a feat, like winning a gold medal, feels like standing at the crest of a magnificent wave. Both experiences, though vastly different, teach us the same truth: life is ever-changing. Grief softens with time, allowing cherished memories to shine brighter, while triumph becomes a cherished milestone, a testament to resilience and effort. Embracing this ebb and flow empowers you to honor both sorrow and joy, knowing that every moment—whether filled with pain or pride—is part of the tide that shapes who you are and carries you forward toward growth and new possibilities.

When my Holy Cross basketball jersey was retired—among the first wave of women's basketball players to receive the honor—I closed my tear-filled speech with a heartfelt sentiment: "I can imagine my dad and Togo watching together in heaven from the front row." Even now, that image never fails to bring a smile to my face.

Letter to Your Future Self (or Younger Self)

> *We are living this season with a growth mindset, always examining ourselves through the lens of improvement—focusing on how we can grow, what areas need attention, and creating actionable steps to get better every day. What is next? Where do you see yourself at the end of the game? The season? The year? And beyond?*
>
> *Now, take a moment to reflect: What would you say to your future self? If you were to write a letter, what wisdom would you include? Would you remind yourself that the time spent worrying about points or stats was wasted energy? Would you emphasize the value of showing up every day and giving your absolute best? Or perhaps you'd affirm that hard work truly does pay off in the end.*
>
> *When you establish a pattern of reflection and revelation, turn those insights into motivation and action, and then cap it off with honest evaluation, your story becomes one of success and growth. The game, just like life, is your template—a blank page waiting for you to write your happy ending!*

WRITING A REFLECTION letter to your future self is a powerful way to capture your current thoughts, goals, and emotions while offering a unique opportunity for self-growth. It allows you to articulate where you are in life right now—your dreams, challenges, and priorities—so that your future self can look back and see how far you've come.

We would write this at the beginning of the season and read it near the end. Though it was just a few months, it was fascinating to see how dreams were realized.

When I was competing for the Boston Blazers AAU team in 1978 in

Kansas City, Missouri, we finished in fifth place. It was a huge accomplishment for a team from New England to place in the top six. In those days, the meccas of basketball were Tennessee, California, and Pennsylvania.

For additional context, in those days, there was one national tournament called the National Junior Olympic Championship. There was one AAU team that I was on in all of New England. Our roster included twelve future All-Americans. Nowadays, there may be thousands of AAU programs in Massachusetts alone.

We were on a hot streak, and our talent was good enough to land us in the game for the fifth-place medal. Our opponent, the team from Southern California, included now Hall of Famers the McGee twins and Cheryl Miller. The game would be fought till the end, with my role focused on defense rather than offense. We would win, garner the fifth-place medal!

Unfortunately, there was one player on our team who didn't get into the game. She was devastated and crying after the game. It was a huge win for our New England program, and the coach admittedly forgot to put her in the game at the end. As we all celebrated with our families in the stands and with our teammates in the locker room, Mary was a bit aloof. I felt bad for her and her family, who made the trip to see her compete.

Later that day, she had gathered herself, and when we were chilling in the lobby of the hotel, I asked how she was doing. She said she was doing better after talking with her parents. She relayed to me what they had told her, "If a problem isn't going to matter in five years or more, don't spend more than five minutes being upset by it." It's actually a famous saying, but I didn't know this at the time. I do remember that when she said it, and it made complete sense. We stress about things in the moment that most likely will not have any bearing on our lives in the future. So, imagine what your letter would look like and what advice you would give your younger self or future self.

WOWsdom! The Girls' Guide to the Positive and the Possible is a book that the company I work for, Generation W, and its founder, Donna Orender, published. Donna is one of my mentors and, more importantly, a dear friend. She is incredibly intelligent, an unbelievable wordsmith, who fuels her soul with helping others. I am blessed and so grateful to have her in my life. *WOWsdom* is a beautiful compilation of letters written by suc-cessful women of all ages and experiences to their younger selves. It also has younger girls' letters written to their future selves. Each letter contributes meaningful lessons seen through their lens of experience, timeless wisdom, and hope for a better future. I was honored to have my letter published in the book. Here is an excerpt from my letter:

> *First, let me say, "Way to go!" It's been a part of your nature*
> *to try to succeed and excel at everything you dig into to do…*
> *It has not always been easy to put your head above the crowd.*
> *In fact, it can be downright lonely at times. My parents*
> *used to say, "When you put your head above the crowd,*
> *people will try to knock it off." Somewhat cynical, but true.*
> *It's not your fault that some teammates treat you poorly*
> *because they are jealous of your success—that is on them. The*
> *day you were not voted captain of the basketball team felt*
> *like a dagger to the heart. Through the pain and tears, you*
> *could not have known that that moment was a defining one*
> *for you. You showed up every day, determined to be your best*
> *and follow the advice of your parents to turn it around and*
> *make it a positive life lesson. You find the courage to stay the*
> *course and later in life follow your passion for coaching so*
> *that you can make a difference in the lives of others.*
> *Stay loyal and trustworthy. Continue to befriend those who*
> *eat alone or don't seem to have many friends. It comes back*
> *to you in spades. Your compassion will continue through*
> *life as you mature and then impart that quality to your*
> *daughter (Yes, you will be blessed with a loving daughter).*
> *Loyalty is an amazing quality to have to share with others,*
> *which is a reason your close friends have been with you*
> *for decades. Best advice: Surround yourself with positive-*
> *minded people!*
> *When later on in life you have to deal with the worst kind*
> *of adversity—being told those four words, "You have*

breast cancer," you keep looking through your positive lens. Battling cancer was by far the worst ordeal in your life that you had to endure. Your determination and your support system, surrounding yourself with like-minded strong people, will help you to conquer this and create a new lens to help others.

Finally, stay true to who you are—go ALL IN in any endeavor you take on. Your loving family, amazing experiences, and dear friends build a strong foundation for you to invest, reap dividends, and paint within the lines.

Love,
Your future self

So give it a try... It doesn't have to be perfect! Forget about proper punctuation or flawless sentence structure; this is a fun and meaningful exercise to reflect and connect with your past while keeping an eye on your future.

525,600 Minutes

My eight years of playing the clarinet instilled in me a deep appreciation for music, from the timeless elegance of classical compositions to the vibrant storytelling of Broadway. If you're familiar with the musical *Rent*, you know its iconic anthem, "Seasons of Love." The 525,600 minutes it references symbolize the moments in a year—each one an opportunity to live fully.

On the way to our NEPSAC Championship game in 2003, Marcia and I were driving to Worcester Academy, listening to her *Broadway Kids* CD, and that song came on. The lyrics resonated differently that day, stirring something deep within me. And just like that, I found my pre-game speech. It was simple: I urged the team to savor every one of the thirty-two minutes on the court, knowing those moments would stay with us forever.

Life's most profound moments often come unexpectedly. Sure, we anticipate milestones like births, graduations, weddings, and bar or bat mitzvahs. But I'm talking about the ones you don't see coming. It's the small, unplanned acts of kindness, the fleeting connections with strangers, and the moments of pure joy that take you by surprise. When we keep our eyes, minds, and hearts open, we allow these extraordinary moments to shape us.

We all have a limited number of minutes on this earth. What you choose to do with your 525,600 minutes every year is a decision you make each day. Use them wisely.

Fast forward twenty years: "You got this!" "Love the burn!" "Every stroke is one stroke closer to the finish line!" These were the mantras that carried me through as our We Can Row Boston crew took on the 2024 Head of the Charles Regatta. The 5K course is a daunting challenge, and our boat—a crew of eight breast cancer survivors, with an average age of sixty-four (I was sixty-two at the time)—was determined to face it together. As we like to say, "We're the best group you never want to be a part of!"

My journey into rowing began after I just finished breast cancer treatment. Or what I refer to as my nine months of hell. My daughter, who rowed for Community Rowing (CRI), spotted a flyer for We Can Row Boston seeking new members and urged me to give it a try. I had never rowed before, but with Marcia's encouragement, I thought, *Why not?* I filled out the paperwork, passed the swim test, got my doctor's approval, and showed up for my first session.

A legendary rower, Holly Metcalf, is a six-time USA national and Olympic team member in women's rowing, who won a gold medal in rowing at the 1984 Summer Olympics for the women's eight, and is the founder of this extraordinary organization for breast cancer survivors to "re-build physical strength and mental focus." Holly once said, "We row with the sum of our strength."

Dressed in baggy basketball shorts and a T-shirt, I quickly learned rowing demanded specialized gear, like rowing tights to prevent my clothes from catching in the sliding seat! Despite my initial nerves, I fell in love with the sport. My coaches, Molly, a former national champion at Washington State University, and Alice, were endlessly encouraging and patient with me. I was so grateful to have a coach like Molly, who welcomed me into a new sport with open arms, patiently taught me rowing's demanding techniques, and helped me discover something that gave me back the confidence cancer treatments had taken away.

Rowing gave me a new challenge, a fresh sport to learn, and a way to reclaim my strength after the grueling ordeal of surgery, chemo, and radiation. Most importantly, it connected me with a group of women who truly understood what I had endured. This passion for rowing and its community grew so deeply that I took on leadership roles, serving as a board member, vice president, and eventually president of We Can Row Boston.

In 2024, we finally had our chance to row in an exhibition race in the Head of the Charles Regatta on behalf of the Survivors Rowing Network. Eleven cancer survivor boats from across the world gathered, including teams from Italy, France, Germany, and cities like Chicago, Philadelphia, and Washington, DC.

On a warm New England day, with my daughter and friends cheering from the famous Weeks Bridge over the Charles River, we completed the course in under twenty-four minutes. For some, that time might seem slow. But for us, it was a resounding triumph. We finished! We did it!

What I love most about rowing is its demand for perfect synchronization. Each rower must move in unison with the person in front of them—handle height, shoulder turn, leg bend, the catch—everything must align. Not that we ever reach this perfection, but we show up ready to try. Training mostly twice a week with my crew taught us not just how to row but how to trust one another and offer support when doubts crept in. In an eight-person shell, there are no timeouts and no substitutions. Success depends entirely on collective effort.

There's a unique, almost indescribable thrill in the rhythm of rowing—gliding across the water, the oar cutting cleanly with each synchronized stroke. It's a sport that demands raw strength, exacting precision, and above all, complete trust in your teammates. In rowing, you quickly learn that success doesn't come from individual effort—it comes from unity. Together, you move. Together, you push through pain. Together, you reach the finish.

The film *The Boys in the Boat*, based on the true story of the 1936 US Olympic men's rowing team, captures this beautifully. Watching those young men triumph in Berlin against all odds was deeply moving. One line from the film stayed with me: "When all eight are rowing in perfect unison, rowing becomes more poetry than sport." That line doesn't just describe rowing—it defines it. It's beautiful. It's true. And it reminds us that when we move in harmony with others, we can achieve something far greater than ourselves.

The hours of training and the preparation we endured were nothing compared to what we had faced during breast cancer treatments yet there were times that we all relied on those grueling moments that had already proven what we were capable of.

The 23:53, how long it took to row the Head of the Charles course, and a small part of my 2024's 525,600 minutes, will remain with me forever—a testament to resilience, teamwork, and the strength we find in each other.

Bucket list...check!

Get To vs. Have To

Think about how you went about your day today. Did you wake up and say to yourself, "Ugh,, I have to go to school?" Or "I have to take a quiz in Spanish class?" Or even "I have to sit on the bench again today?"

Change one word in those sentences and you will change your entire view. "I GET to go to school." Girls in some countries are prevented from going to school. "I GET to take a quiz in Spanish class." Think about the opportunity to prove your knowledge of another language and how hard you studied. "I GET to sit on the bench today." Wow, you are a part of something bigger than yourself; a team that has the potential to win a championship, and you are still learning.

Today, you GET to compete, proudly representing your school community, and have a chance to do your best!

How often do you catch yourself thinking about all the things you "have to do" in a day?

"I have to go to the supermarket."

"I have to go to work."

"I have to call my mom."

"I have to eat healthy."

The list goes on and on, creating a constant undercurrent of obligation and stress.

But what if you replaced "have to" with "get to"?

"I *get to* go to the supermarket and buy fresh food."

"I *get to* go to work and earn a living."

"I *get to* call my mom and hear her voice."

"I *get to* choose nutritious food that fuels my body."

That small change in language can transform how you see your responsibilities, turning them from burdens into privileges. It's a subtle shift, but it carries the power to spark gratitude and reframe your day-to-day experiences.

Gratitude isn't just about feeling good—it's scientifically proven to make a real difference in your life. Research has shown that practicing gratitude can improve overall well-being, boost resilience, strengthen social connections, and reduce stress and depression. The more you focus on what you *get to* do, the more your mindset will align with appreciation and positivity.

So, the next time you find yourself overwhelmed by your to-do list, pause for a moment and reframe it. What do you *get to* do today? You might be surprised by how much joy and fulfillment you uncover.

The mind is an incredibly powerful tool, and understanding its potential is key to unlocking success. When I speak to teams about the concept that mindset is a muscle, I like to use the example of shooting a free throw. Think about it: If you shoot a free throw in the first minute of the game, it feels different from shooting one with only 1.4 seconds left in a tied game. What changes? The shot itself remains the same—same distance, same form—but the situation shifts. The pressure doesn't come from the physical aspects of the shot; it comes from the mental perspective you bring to it.

The difference is in how your mind responds. The body can perform the same motion, but it's the mind that either adds pressure or eases it. The mental strength to stay calm under pressure, focus, and trust your training is what makes all the difference. This is why mindset, like any muscle, must be conditioned and strengthened through practice, just like any physical skill.

When I was ten, my sister and I spent seven weeks at Camp Wyoda in Fairlee, Vermont. It was a recommendation from a friend's mom, who worked as the camp nurse, and my parents saw it as a perfect way for us to stay active over the summer. We were fortunate to attend, and I remember it as a truly glorious time. To this day, those are some of my fondest memories.

At Camp Wyoda, I dove into everything—from tennis to sailing, canoeing to archery. Hiking trips, campfires, and laughter with friends were a constant. Over the next nine summers, I would grow deeply connected to the camp and its community. In fact, some of my closest friends today are fellow Wyodians. Those years remain some of the happiest, most carefree moments of my life. Back then, the emphasis wasn't on specializing in a single sport. Instead, we were encouraged to develop in multiple activities, building strength and balance in body and mind.

It was a time to simply be, to spend hours with friends, laugh, play pranks, be silly, and be outdoors. Fun pranks like hiding our friend Kiki's bugle mouthpiece so we could get a few more minutes of sleep. (You really did it this time, Kiki!!) Or short-sheet our counselor's bed on her day off. We even pranked the upper bunks by hiding a cassette player in the woods with a recording of us earlier running out of the cabin after taps.

However, as basketball became my passion and the dream of playing in college grew stronger, I began to realize that attending Camp Wyoda each summer was potentially hindering my skill development. Wyoda didn't have a basketball court. Seven weeks without a basketball in my hands felt like an eternity. But rather than letting that stop me, I found a way to make it work.

Most mornings, at 7:00 a.m.—thirty minutes before reveille, the bugle call that woke us up like an alarm clock signaling the start of the day—I would *get to* jog along the winding camp roads for two miles, dribbling a basketball as I went. I would *get to* witness the mist rise from the lake, hear the birds greet the dawn, and push myself to improve my ball-handling skills with crossovers, speed dribbles, and spins. The sound of the ball bouncing against the hills echoed across camp, and my friends often joked years later about those "morning thumps."

They would question my dedication, teasing, "Why get up early every day to run? Just sleep in." But looking back, I realize I didn't *have to*—I *got to*. I got to make the most of every moment, to find a way to stay committed to my goals, and to embrace the challenges that helped me grow.

Changing how you think about responsibility can be incredibly freeing. When you shift from feeling like you *have to* do something to recognizing that you *get to*, you realize just how much lighter the load becomes. The weight of obligation lifts, and what once felt like a burden becomes an opportunity.

Do It for Someone Else!

> *When you step onto the court today, dedicate every play to someone who matters deeply to you. Picture them sitting in the gym or watching online, cheering you on. Play not just for yourself or your teammates but for that person who inspires you to give your all.*
>
> *When the fourth quarter comes and your lungs burn, your legs feel heavy, and the game tests your resolve, think of them.*
>
> *Let their presence fuel you to push harder, to keep going, and to give everything you've got. When the final buzzer sounds, walk off the court knowing you gave it your all—knowing you made them proud.*

By dedicating your efforts to someone else, whether it's a loved one, a cause, or a larger community, you can find a sense of purpose and fulfillment beyond your expectations. Working toward the accountability of others can provide a deep sense of meaning in your actions and give you a reason to strive for excellence.

You will be investing time, energy, and resources into thinking beyond yourself. It's amazing how much more you can find in the tank when you are doing it for someone else. Picture that person in your mind's eye when times are tough and see how far you can go. Knowing that your efforts have positively influenced someone else's life can be deeply rewarding.

I discussed earlier my tongue depressor activity in my pre-game speech, "Stronger Together," in the First Quarter section of this book, when I asked my players to write down who they would dedicate the season to. This is an additional affirmation to remind oneself of their dedication to others which often requires selflessness, empathy, and the development of valuable skills. It can push you to expand your capabilities, learn new things, and step outside your comfort zone. Through your efforts to assist and support others, you may also gain new perspectives, increase your emotional intelligence, and enhance your problem-solving abilities.

My playing career at Holy Cross profoundly shaped the person I am today. The dedication I poured into perfecting my basketball skills is a source of pride, and the grit and resilience I developed through overcoming challenges laid the foundation for my success in life and managing challenging times. Looking back to Togo and "doing it for someone else," my intention never wavered. Through it all, I remained true to one thing: my authentic self.

My former teammate and good friend, Kim, reminded me of something truly special before the incredible honor of having the Sherry Levin Women's Locker Room named after me in 2021. Back in 1983, Kim was a freshman point guard during my senior year at Holy Cross, and we bonded instantly. She was an intense competitor, a kind and supportive teammate, and someone who made everyone around her better. Kim was happy to pass me the ball without a hint of jealousy, as I led the team in scoring and was bound to get Kim an assist. Kim was a winner not only on the court, but off. As a captain, I took her under my wing—not just as a mentor, but as a friend.

Over the years, Kim and I have stayed in touch, often sharing conversations about basketball and our families. Even as we age and discuss our continued journeys through life, she gives me inspiration: "Find your joy in hunting for your purpose." Profound indeed.

When she called to congratulate me on my locker room honor, she said something that took me by surprise. She shared with me, "As great as you were on the court, you were an even better person off the court." Wow. I was deeply moved. I got a little choked up, thanked her, and asked what had prompted her to say that.

Kim then shared a memory from her freshman year. At the time, she was struggling to balance Holy Cross's rigorous academics with the demands of basketball—practicing six or seven days a week, traveling for games, and trying to keep up with classes. Nervous about approaching a senior, she asked me for advice. For me, the decision to help her was a no-brainer. I invited her to my dorm room and walked her through how I managed my daily priorities using a handwritten calendar and a to-do list—this was 1983, long before smartphones and digital tools. Kim remembers being so grateful for my time and guidance. But to me, it was simply something I would always do.

What I couldn't have anticipated was how much that small act of kindness would impact her. Kim went on to become a successful lawyer and executive, and we remain grateful for the friendship and love we share. Together, we uphold a similar philosophy: to be good people while staying true to ourselves.

I often think about my dad driving me to AAU practices, my parents sitting in the stands for every game, and their unwavering support as a constant source of strength. I think of my grandmother, who knew next to nothing about basketball but still cheered passionately for her "Sherrella." I think of my mom, always finding ways to support me, no matter what. And I think of my daughter, who looks up to me with eyes and a heart full of trust and admiration. Marcia is my rock and my sunshine. For them, there's simply no way I could ever give less than my absolute best.

That's why I chose to conclude *Pre-Game* with this particular speech—it has the power to create a deeply meaningful and transformative experience for any team. Pushing yourself to be your best is commendable, but dedicating your effort to someone else takes it to another level entirely. It introduces a sense of purpose that transcends personal goals, turning effort into a tribute and determination into devotion.

When you exist not just for yourself but for the people who believe in you, you tap into a deeper well of motivation. It's not just about avoiding disappointment—it's about honoring the trust and love they've given you.

That's a force strong enough to inspire greatness.

In the end, having a positive mindset isn't just about staying upbeat or pushing through tough days—it's about choosing to live with intention, to show up fully not just for yourself, but for others. It's about finding strength not only within but with the help of others, joy in purpose, and meaning in the relationships that shape us. When you root your mindset in gratitude, dedication, and the quiet power of selflessness, you begin to see that true success isn't measured by wins or accolades, but by the lives you touch and the impact you make.

Creating my pre-game speeches set the tone for all that basketball and life have to offer. That's the mindset I hoped to inspire: one grounded in heart, fueled by purpose, and anchored in something far greater than the scoreboard.

That's where real dedication happens—and where lasting impact begins.

A POST-GAME GUIDE TO CREATING YOUR WINNING MINDSET BOOK

Thanks for reading!

Pre-Game: A Winning Mindset is meant to do what every great pre-game speech does: fire you up, bring people together, and spark conversations that lead to growth, connection, positivity, and lasting change. The lessons in these pages become even more powerful when they're shared. When teammates, classmates, colleagues, families, or book clubs sit down to discuss these stories, something shifts, and you begin to see how resilience, authenticity, and perseverance play out not only in sports but also in everyday life.

Think of these prompts as your post-game huddle. They're designed to help you go beyond the words on the page and explore in a new lens how the ideas here connect with your own journey. Whether you're an athlete preparing for the next big game, a coach shaping tomorrow's leaders, a parent supporting a child's dreams, or a professional navigating setbacks and opportunities, this is your chance to bring the lessons off the page and into action.

And perhaps, like I've done, you'll start to see everything through the lens of a pre-game speech: a pause to reflect, a reset to regain focus, and a push forward with courage, clarity, and heart.

—Sherry Levin

For Athletes and Teams

This is your chance to practice the positive mindset muscle together. Use these questions to push yourselves the way you would in training.

- ✓ Which pre-game speech resonated most with you, and why?
- ✓ How do you personally "get in the zone" before a game? How does it compare with the strategies in this book?
- ✓ Think back to a time you faced a setback in sports. What mindset tools helped you push through? Or what tools from this book could have helped?
- ✓ "Mindset is a muscle" is a central theme. What are three daily habits your team could adopt to strengthen it?
- ✓ When you stop to think about a particular thing that happened to you, big or small, try to reframe it into a positive motivation.
- ✓ If your team were to create its own pre-game speech, what would it sound like?

For Coaches and Leaders

Every coach has a playbook—this one is about mindset. Use these prompts to sharpen your leadership and remind yourself of the kind of mentor you want to be.

- ✓ How do you define your leadership style? How does it align with my focus on authenticity, resilience, and connection?
- ✓ Which of the metaphors could you use with your own team or group?
- ✓ How do you balance accountability with compassion?
- ✓ In what ways can coaches cultivate mental toughness while also encouraging vulnerability?
- ✓ What story or speech in this book reminded you most of your own leadership journey?
- ✓ Create your own positive message that sets the stage for your team before a game. Remember, your pre-game speech t remains in your players' minds before the start and all through the contest.

For Parents of Athletes

You're on the sidelines, but your impact is in every play. These questions help you reflect on how you guide, support, and inspire your child.

- ✓ How do you support your child through both wins and losses?
- ✓ What lessons from sports do you most hope your child carries into life beyond the game?
- ✓ When do you find it hardest to step back and let your child learn through failure?
- ✓ Which story in the book reminded you of your own child's challenges or triumphs?
- ✓ How might this book change the way you talk to your child before or after a game?

For Professionals and Leaders

The boardroom, the classroom, the office—it's all an arena. Use these questions to think about how you prepare yourself for life's biggest moments.

- ✓ Which pre-game speech or quarter felt most relevant to your professional or personal challenges?
- ✓ How do you train your positive mindset muscle in your career or daily life?
- ✓ What's your version of the "green sneaker debate"—a moment when your stubbornness or conviction shaped your path? When has your authentic self played a role in making a big decision?
- ✓ How do you build resilience in the workplace when setbacks or losses occur?
- ✓ If you were to write your own locker room challenge for your peers, what would it be?

For General Book Clubs and Readers

Even if you've never played or coached, the lessons here apply to navigating life. These questions can help you uncover what resonated most for you.

- ✓ Which story made you laugh? Which one made you cry?
- ✓ How did my willingness to be vulnerable—sharing tears, stubbornness, and cheesy habits—shape the way you connected with me?

✓ What role has sports (as an athlete, fan, or parent) played in your life?

✓ Did the book shift how you think about resilience or authenticity?

✓ What is one "pre-game" mindset you want to adopt in your own life after reading this book?

Group Activity

End your discussion with a challenge: Have each reader write a one-minute pre-game speech to the group. Share them aloud and reflect together on the values and lessons that matter most.

Illustration by Susan Schön

"Always dream and shoot
Higher than you know you can do.
Don't bother to just be better than
Your competitors.
Try to be better than yourself."

—**William Faulkner**

ABOUT THE AUTHOR

Sherry Levin is a trailblazer whose four-decade career spans elite athletics, transformative coaching, media production, and motivational leadership. As a Performance Strategist and Leadership Success Coach, she has dedicated her career to helping individuals and organizations unlock their full potential through mental toughness, resilience, and strategic thinking.

Sherry's journey began on the basketball court at Holy Cross College, where she became the first woman to receive a full athletic scholarship and the all-time leading scorer in women's basketball—an achievement that earned her a place in the Holy Cross Hall of Fame and the honor of having the *Sherry Levin Women's Basketball Lounge* named in her tribute, along with her retired jersey. Her athletic excellence extended beyond college, leading to inductions into the Newton North High School Hall of Fame, the New England Basketball Hall of Fame, and the Jewish Heritage Athletic Hall of Fame.

As a coach, Sherry compiled an extraordinary 420-97 record with an 81% winning percentage, including five New England Championships and two undefeated seasons. Her coaching prowess took her to the international stage, where she led Team USA to five gold medals across the World Maccabiah Games. Among her many mentees is Aliyah Boston, the #1 WNBA draft pick and 2023 Rookie of the Year, a testament to Sherry's ability to develop championship-level talent.

Beyond the court, Sherry has made her mark as an ESPN analyst and creative leader in video production, bringing her unique perspective on performance and leadership to broader audiences. As a sought-after motivational speaker, she captivates audiences with authentic stories drawn from her experiences as a single mother and breast cancer survivor—challenges that deepened her understanding of resilience and shaped her philosophy that mindset is the foundation of all success.

Today, Sherry's signature **"Mindset is a Muscle"** program serves as the cornerstone of her work with teams and organizations. Through dynamic workshops and keynote sessions, she teaches leaders how to strengthen their mental fortitude, elevate their leadership capabilities, and create cultures of sustained excellence. Her approach combines decades of elite coaching experience with practical strategies that drive transformation, helping individuals and teams lead with clarity, confidence, and purpose.

Sherry Levin's life and work embody the power of positivity, teamwork, and unwavering determination. Whether on the court, in the boardroom, or on stage, she continues to inspire others to push beyond their limits and achieve extraordinary results.